David Lampe
May '92

Donald R. Howard

Writers and Pilgrims
Medieval Pilgrimage Narratives and Their Posterity

University of California Press

Berkeley · Los Angeles · London

Library of Congress Catalog Card Number: 79-64480
ISBN 0-520-03926-2

University of California Press
Berkeley and Los Angeles, California

University of California Press, Ltd.
London, England

Printed in the United States of America

1 2 3 4 5 6 7 8 9

To Morton W. Bloomfield
and Christian K. Zacher,
two of my unofficial teachers

Contents

Acknowledgments

This is an aerial view of a forgotten genre: ordinary writings that rose naturally from a medieval institution and became a literary form with its own posterity.

My research began in 1968 with a question: were there any factual accounts of medieval pilgrimages that show us how Chaucer would have expected a pilgrimage to be described? I didn't know of any such works and was surprised to find that there were many hundreds. Some parts of the present book were first written with another one in mind, so I must acknowledge again my debts to the John Simon Guggenheim Memorial Foundation, to friends and colleagues who read earlier versions, and to numerous libraries, especially the British Library and the New York Public. What was relevant to my argument in *The Idea of the Canterbury Tales* (1976) was compressed there into a few pages. What I wrote about Mandeville was published in *The Yearbook of English Studies* 1 (1971): 1–17, in a rather different version, and I am grateful to the Modern Humanities Research Association, publisher of that journal, for allowing me to reprint here those paragraphs that remain the same. I went on reading other pilgrimage writings as I could lay hands on them, but there are many more than I have read. To read them all and read the best with care would be a life's work, one I could recommend to some future scholar for its interest. I haven't meant to do more in this small book than introduce the subject.

I'm grateful to Barry Ahearn for his help and advice in checking references and revising. The manuscript was read by James Dean, U. C. Knoepflmacher, and Christian K. Zacher, and by my colleagues at Stanford, George Dekker and Paul Robinson; I am grateful to all for their suggestions, and to Robert Watson for his help and counsel in preparing the index.

Translations are mine unless otherwise noted.

1.
The Mirrors of Future Times

On an autumn afternoon in 1797, having taken two grains of opium, Samuel Taylor Coleridge, critic and bard, woke from a three-hour sleep to recall a poem composed in his dreams, and "instantly and eagerly" began to write. So at least he reported some eighteen years later. Interrupted by a "person on business from Porlock," he could remember no more of the poem that had seemed two or three hundred lines long, and the resulting fragment, "Kubla Khan," was published (but not until 1816) with a note telling the strange story of its composition. In modern times everything about the story—the year, the opium, the dream, the memory, the alliterative person from Porlock—has been called into question, everything except the one detail with which we are to be concerned: the book he was reading when he fell asleep.

The book was *Purchas His Pilgrimage, or Relations of the World and the Religions Observed in All Ages and Places discovered, from the Creation unto this Present* (1613). On his own testimony, Coleridge had the book open to a passage that reads:

In Xamdu did Cublai Can build a stately Palace, encompassing sixteene miles of plaine ground with a wall, wherein are fertile Meddowes, pleasant springs, delightfull Streames, and all sorts of beasts of chase and game, and in the middest thereof a sumptuous house of pleasure, which may be removed from place to place.

Whatever else may be true or false, there is no doubt about the relationship of this passage to the famous verses. They came out of his reading. And because this at least cannot be doubted, generations of scholars have pored over every phrase in the poem, attempting to show what verbal scraps it was made of and by what process they were put together. Whether the poet assembled half-remembered phrases in associative patterns, like "hooks and eyes"; whether for neurotic or promotional reasons he fabricated the opium dream; whether he fantasized and reported such a dream under the full tilt of a romantic vogue, or made the poem in the larger sway of his plans to write an apocalyptic epic called "The Fall of Jerusalem"—none of this need concern us. However the poem was written and whatever it means, it is a classic instance of the maxim that literary works are made out of other literary works. In a great moment of literary history, something Coleridge read, a book almost two centuries old in his time, came to be transformed into something he wrote—in this instance, a masterpiece.

For Coleridge and his contemporaries, books like Purchas's were a telescope in which to view a gone world. In the early seventeenth century, the earth not yet wholly mapped, scholars like Samuel Purchas and his predecessor Richard Hakluyt were gathering accounts by travellers for clues and wonders, like tales of outer space. Among such travellers—explorers, merchants, missionaries—were pilgrims to the Holy Land: not a large number, for Jerusalem was to the geographer but one of many places. But the pilgrimage remained a favored *image* of travel, and Purchas chose that image for the titles of all three of his books.[1] In Purchas's time the Jerusalem pilgrimage was a thing of the past, not just in Protestant England where it would have been reckoned a popish custom, but in Catholic Europe too: it had, with its cognate institutions (relics, Crusades), passed out of fashion. What was *written* about the medieval pilgrimages, however, survived: it was still interesting to read old tales of shrines and marvels, descriptions of distant lands and exotic customs. And such books, still on shelves, enjoyed a readership not just in the seventeenth century, when the New World was still largely unexplored, but well after that—in Coleridge's day and throughout his century. To Coleridge and his poetical friends, such books were a powerful stimulus. They read them for wonder and imagery more than for knowledge—books like Purchas's *Pilgrimage* and *Pilgrims,* and *Mandeville's Travels* (a great favorite of Coleridge's), alongside dozens of seventeenth- and eighteenth-century accounts of voyages to the New World. With such works, one writer observes, "the printed page

1. Apart from the *Pilgrimage,* which appeared in three other, enlarged editions during his lifetime (the fourth in 1626), Purchas's other titles, to the reader's confusion, are *Purchas His Pilgrim: Microcosmos, or the History of Man* (1619) and *Hakluytus Posthumus, or Purchas His Pilgrimes, Contayning a History of the World in Sea Voyages and Lande Travells by Englishmen and others* (1625).

and the reader's imagination effect an alchemy to which television cannot aspire; a viewer might watch an entire series of programmes on the Arctic and yet never once receive an impression so brilliant and un-forgettable as this glimpse of penguins given by Narborough: 'they are short-legged like a Goose, and stand upright like little Children in White Aprons, in companies together.'"[2]

At the turn of our century, such reading matter began to gather dust. It is now almost unknown. If we read Chaucer or Dante, we suppose that the realistic Canterbury pilgrimage, or Dante's more spiritual pilgrimage to Beatrice, must have had a background in medieval writings.[3] But no such writings are a part of our tradition of reading, not even the famous English book written in Chaucer's time, *Mandeville's Travels,* in its day and for five centuries known all over Europe.

What were such writings like? How many were there and how widely were they read? What influence, if any, did they have on literature? What use are they as background? Asking such questions first with Chaucer's pilgrimage in mind, I saw that this large, forgotten body of writings has something to reveal

2. Molly Lefebure, *Samuel Taylor Coleridge: A Bondage of Opium* (New York: Stein and Day, 1974), p. 181.

3. About this I had my brief say in *The Idea of the Canterbury Tales* (Berkeley and Los Angeles: University of California Press, 1976), pp. 28–30 and passim. For previous studies, all of which deal however with the pilgrimage as metaphor rather than as institution, see below, ch. 4, n. 3. On Dante, John G. Demaray, *The Invention of Dante's "Commedia"* (New Haven: Yale University Press, 1974), deals with the institution and the actual journey in Dante's consciousness, not with literary properties of pilgrimage writings.

about the rise of fiction, of satire, of the novel; about the context of medieval literature, not just in its own day but in later eras; and about the context of English literature up until about the time of Pound.

I have been calling the books "writings," not in any cold spirit as one might talk of leavings, but in a neutral way, as one would talk of paintings. It is a convention of our century to count as the literature of our time only writings that were written as literature, but to count as the literature of previous centuries all we deem worthy of the name: Johnson's preface to his dictionary, the *Spectator,* any number of letters, reviews, diaries, articles are called literature because we like to read them. Not to mention the tiresome verses or creaky plays and novels included for historical reasons as part of "the background." Most of the medieval accounts of pilgrimages might fall into that category, but the best—whether fact or fiction—are literature by any sensible definition. They deserve to be read. They were the products of their authors' ability to lend luster—"to portray," as Vladimir Nabokov put it, "ordinary objects as they will be reflected in the kindly mirrors of future times."

We are concerned then with a "body" of writings; but in their own time they were not that. A man of Chaucer's day might have known of a few such works, but no one could have suspected there were many hundreds. A guidebook for pilgrims would go out of date. A journal of a pilgrimage would have only local currency; some may never have been read outside the town in which they were written. A few authors gained reputations, and their books were widely

known: Jacques de Vitry's *History of Jerusalem,* Boldensele's *Itinerarium, Mandeville's Travels.* But some of
the masterpieces of pilgrimage literature were barely
known until the nineteenth century. For us—with our
catalogues and bibliographies, our historical (one
could say scientific) capability of anatomizing, listing
such works by author, place, time, manner of
treatment—they are a body, like other such bodies of
medieval writings having a common subject: like
works on the "virtues and vices," "contempt of the
world," "the art of dying." We can call the body a
genre, but when we draw up close we will see sub-
classes: logs, guides, and narrations.

Not only these writings but the *image* of the pilgrimage kept a place in European thought into the
nineteenth century. The pilgrimage itself, dead as an
institution in England by the end of the sixteenth century, lived on as an idea preserved in books. There was
never a time when the words *pilgrim* and *pilgrimage*
didn't have force, and as we shall see they connoted a
one-way journey to a destination, made for a purpose
worthy of reverence. Purchas's use of the word in his
titles already shows secularization: his pilgrims' purpose was to return home with knowledge. And, of
course, Bunyan's *The Pilgrim's Progress* comes at once
to mind. In such allegories, as in spiritual guides and
autobiographies of the period, the individual Christian's internal struggle in the world was reckoned a
pilgrimage—the image is discernible in *Robinson
Crusoe.*[4] For, as was always true, *pilgrimage* was a

4. See J. Paul Hunter, *The Reluctant Pilgrim: Defoe's Emblematic
Method and Quest for Form in "Robinson Crusoe"* (Baltimore: Johns
Hopkins Press, 1966), esp. pp. 89–128, 195, 201.

metaphor for human life: life is a one-way passage to the Heavenly Jerusalem and we are pilgrims on it. In the eighteenth century, the metaphor of the pilgrimage never disappeared, but it was in various texts supplanted or augmented by other images, especially that of life as theater: this image allowed the author to be not a returned traveller and omniscient narrator but a privileged spectator, exploring personages in relation to one another and to the world, uncovering their masks and roles—an important step in the history of fiction. [5]

Between medieval and modern times the image of the pilgrimage underwent a change that easily escapes notice: it came to have turning points and crossroads, and a return. To us, with works like Bunyan's in mind, the "pilgrimage of life" is marked off by moral crises and choices; its goal is growth in character. This was true in medieval writings when the full allegorical implications were drawn out, as in a work like Deguileville's *Pélérinage de la vie humaine*. But a medieval pilgrimage was essentially a matter of staying on the straight road and not "wandering by the way." The associated image of the labyrinth or maze tells us much about this fundamental change. In medieval thought a labyrinth *was* a pilgrimage. You could find a mosaic on the floor of some Gothic cathedrals called a labyrinth or "house of Daedalus." Judging from inscriptions on some of them, they were used as substitute pilgrimages:

5. See Ronald Paulson, "Life as Journey and as Theater: Two Eighteenth-Century Narrative Structures," *New Literary History* 7 (1976): 43–58. On the image in its broadest sense, see Gerhart B. Ladner, "*Homo Viator*: Mediaeval Ideas of Alienation and Order," *Speculum* 42 (1967): 233–259.

the pilgrim could crawl along them on his knees, mov-
ing towards his destination at the center, which was
called *ciel* or *Jérusalem*. They were *unicursal* mazes:
there were many convolutions but no blind choices to
be made—no choices at all. The *multicursal* maze,
where one must take wrong turns and feel one's way
by trial and error, reflects modern ideas about life's
pilgrimage, ideas that involve empiricism and a prefer-
ence for works over grace. In such a maze, one's object
is to get back out. The popularity of these puzzle mazes
seems to date from the end of the seventeenth century.[6]

By the nineteenth century, kinds of journeys which
to the medieval mind would have had little to do with
pilgrimage—the voyage of exploration, the chivalric
quest, the sojourn, even the prodigal's return—had
become conflated. The romantic quest, even when as
with Byron it is *called* a pilgrimage, was a new and
different image: it had become internalized.[7] It was a
journey into the self, and the antagonist was no longer
exterior temptation (as in the Middle Ages) or external
nature (as in Defoe) but identity, selfhood: the roman-

6. See W. H. Mathews, *Mazes and Labyrinths: Their History and
Development* (1922; rpt. New York: Dover, 1970), esp. ch. 9; and
Joan Evans, *Art in Medieval France* (London and New York: Ox-
ford University Press, 1948), pp. 87–112.

7. Georg Roppen and Richard Sommer, *Strangers and Pilgrims:
An Essay on the Metaphor of Journey*, Norwegian Studies in English
no. 11 (Oslo: Akademisk Forlag, 1964), attempts to study the
romantic quest against this background but is itself an example of
the conflation. M. H. Abrams, *Natural Supernaturalism: Tradition
and Revolution in Romantic Literature* (1971; rpt. New York: Norton,
1973), esp. pp. 164–169, 190–195, explores the history of this
conflation in Christian thought.

tics had to shake off selfhood to attain their interior Edens of love and knowledge, of triumphant imagination.[8] From this point of view, "Kubla Khan" has much to do with the travel book Coleridge had been reading. The poem with its attendant story of a vision lost to memory is an internalized quest for a kind of enchantment realized in the poem itself: the poet "on honey-dew hath fed / And drunk the milk of Paradise."[9] It would not be unreasonable to read Coleridge's famous note about his dream as a prose fiction intended to provide the proper imaginative context for reading the poem. The dream is a one-way journey like a pilgrimage, the wakening a return home.

Later in the nineteenth century, though the pilgrimage *per se* no longer found its way into the substance of literature, the medieval accounts of pilgrimages passed to a different and no less avid readership. They became the objects of an international scholarly craze. Most of our knowledge of them comes from the bibliographies, editions, and translations of this period. The vogue passed at the turn of the century, and they were forgotten. In what follows I hope to revive their mem-

8. Harold Bloom, "The Internalization of Quest Romance," in *The Ringers in the Tower: Studies in Romantic Tradition* (Chicago: University of Chicago Press, 1971), pp. 13–35.

9. The phrase is usually glossed as owing to Plato's *Ion,* 533–34, but Josephine Waters Bennett, in *The Rediscovery of Sir John Mandeville* (1954; rpt. New York: Kraus Reprint, 1971), p. 256, argues—whether rightly I do not know—that "Coleridge's 'honey dew' goes back ultimately to Mandeville's account of manna, and his 'milk of paradise' flows from the well in Mandeville's *Travels.*" One might just add that Jerusalem was conventionally called by medieval pilgrims the land of milk and honey.

ory. The brief selective history of these factual
writings, explored in the next chapter for their literary
qualities, leads up to their emergence in imaginative
literature. *Mandeville's Travels* and Chaucer's *Canterbury Tales* are my instances. But the distinction between fact and fiction isn't in this case a strong one.
Travel itself is "imaginative": travels are fictions to the
extent that the traveller sees what he wants or expects
to see, which is often what he has read. Medieval pilgrims in the Holy Land doubtless "really saw" a
crucifix at the center of a banana cut crosswise—and
was that any more outlandish or less real than what *we*
see in a banana? In the last chapter I will suggest some
ways in which these imaginative structures have survived in modern thought.

2.
Writers and Pilgrims

The pilgrimage was one of the most important institutions of late medieval culture; to be more accurate, it was part of a complex of institutions that included the Crusades, the cults of saints, indulgences, relics, and miracles. The ostensible purpose of a pilgrimage was religious—officially it was an act of penance or thanksgiving. From early times it had the metaphorical significance of a one-way journey to the Heavenly Jerusalem: the actual trip was a symbol of human life, and the corollary, that life is a pilgrimage, was a commonplace. The pilgrim enacted the passage from birth to salvation; at his destination he adored the relics of a saint or, at Jerusalem, the places where the Lord had lived and died in his earthly body (and at various shrines worshipped relics of his body presumably not resurrected, like the sweaty image on Saint Veronica's veil preserved at Rome, his milk tooth, his umbilical cord, his blood, or the foreskin from the circumcision, preserved, according to rival claims, in several places). The journey was in part adventure or travel, in part a spiritual exercise or quest; but it was also an actual step on the road to salvation, for part of the gains brought back were indulgences, remissions of the temporal punishment for sin, a practice that began with the Crusades.[1]

The Jerusalem pilgrimage was the pilgrimage of pilgrimages; others were types and shadows of it, for Jerusalem was at the center of the world (it is regularly pictured there in maps of the period), it was the ground the Lord had walked upon, and it was a symbol of the Heavenly City.[2] Other pilgrimages were therefore all in some sense substitutes. At the furthest remove, it was possible to make a substitute pilgrimage by crawling about a cathedral labyrinth; and it was possible to make a pilgrimage by proxy, hiring a pilgrim to travel in one's place.[3] Implicit in the institution itself was the conception of a vicarious pilgrimage.

1. The best study is Jonathan Sumption, *Pilgrimage: An Image of Mediaeval Religion* (Totowa, N.J.: Rowman and Littlefield, 1975), who treats penitential aspects on pp. 98–104, pilgrimages imposed by law on pp. 104–113, pilgrims' vows of thanksgiving on pp. 138–140. On the purpose of pilgrimages, see also Sidney H. Heath, *Pilgrim Life in the Middle Ages* (Boston and New York: Houghton Mifflin, 1912), rpt. and enlarged as *In the Steps of the Pilgrims* (London and New York: Rich and Cowan, 1950), pp. 22, 251–262. On penance and indulgences, Donald J. Hall, *English Mediaeval Pilgrimage* (London: Routledge, 1965), pp. 12–15. On the relics of Christ's body, Sumption, pp. 44–51, and on the relation to Crusades and indulgences, pp. 137, 141–145, 163.

2. The commonplace illustration of the fourfold method of scriptural interpretation was Jerusalem: on the literal level "civitas Judaeorum," on the allegorical "ecclesia Christi," on the tropological "anima hominis," on the anagogical "civitas Dei, illa Coelestis, quae est mater omnium nostrum."

3. Edith Rickert, *Chaucer's World,* ed. C. Olson and M. Crow (New York: Columbia University Press, 1948), pp. 267–268, and Sumption, pp. 295–302.

Jerusalem, then, was a figure, of whose spectral, symbolical quality Norman Cohn has written:

Even for theologians Jerusalem was also a "figure" or symbol of the heavenly city "like unto a stone most precious" which according to the Book of Revelation was to replace it at the end of time. No wonder that—as contemporaries noted—in the minds of simple folk the idea of the earthly Jerusalem became so confused with and transfused by that of the Heavenly Jerusalem that the Palestinian city seemed itself a miraculous realm, abounding both in spiritual and in material blessings. And no wonder that when the masses of the poor set off on their long pilgrimage the children cried out at every town and castle: "Is that Jerusalem?"—while high in the heavens there was seen a mysterious city with vast multitudes hurrying toward it.[4]

This imaginative or figural Jerusalem nevertheless prompted an interest in the real place. The Crusades (themselves a form of pilgrimage) were intended to secure it for Christian pilgrims. The increasing popularity of pilgrimages from the twelfth century on was part of a more general shift in sensibility. In the twelfth century the "angelism" of monastic tradition, in which monks imagined themselves living in imitation of the angels, was supplanted by a devotion to the human Christ. From this period, too, the Crucifix became more and more realistic. The actual places where Christ had lived were objects, too, of this interest in the human or historical side of Christianity.[5]

4. *The Pursuit of the Millennium,* 2nd ed. (New York: Harper and Brothers, 1961), pp. 44–45.

5. Sumption, pp. 92, 135. About the imitation of Christ in

While the pilgrimage was a metaphor for human life and a spiritual exercise, the thing itself was a trip to and back from Jerusalem, Rome, or a particular shrine; so it was travel, which meant danger, adventure, and curiosity. Hence the carnival spirit that moralists frowned upon, and the startling abuses—sexual escapades, for instance, in the dark corners of pilgrims' shrines. Pilgrims returned with more than grace and indulgences to show for their troubles—they had tales to tell, and souvenirs. There were bells, badges, and medallions they could buy, and they were not averse to chipping off bits of stone from the shrines they visited, or (so it was often complained) carving their initials or coats of arms on them. From Jerusalem they brought bottles of muddy Jordan water (powerful against witches), smuggling it past sailors, who believed it caused calms or storms; the twenty-mile trip to Jordan was discouraged by native guides but a must for pilgrims, who would solemnly baptize themselves in its waters or sportively swim in them and at least on one occasion jestingly baptized each other.[6] From Canterbury they brought leaden ampules stamped with St. Thomas's likeness, containing the remarkable holy water on sale there—too powerful for wooden am-

---

monastic tradition I was instructed by Giles Constable in an essay not yet published.

6. Sumption, pp. 129–130. On the sportive conduct, H. F. M. Prescott, *Jerusalem Journey: Pilgrimage to the Holy Land in the Fifteenth Century* (London: Eyre and Spottiswoode, 1954), pp. 151–158; this pleasant book is based on accounts of the pilgrimage organized in 1483, and has been printed in the United States as *Friar Felix at Large: A Fifteenth Century Pilgrimage to the Holy Land* (New Haven: Yale University Press, 1960).

pules, which it was said to split apart. (When we read in Chaucer that English pilgrims sought the martyr who had helped them when they were sick, we assume they had prayed to him, and some assume that the sickness must be spiritual; but it is more likely that they had taken doses of his curative water.)[7] In such ways the pilgrimage reached into all phases of life, subsumed all kinds of human motives, and so was repeatedly regulated and condemned. It was among other things a fine way to escape duty, debt, or the law; King Richard II found it necessary to require anyone on a "far pilgrimage" to obtain "a letters patent under the king's seal, which states the purpose of his journey and the time appointed for his homecoming, *if he is to return.*"[8]

Such a tension between physical act and spiritual intent is present in the whole tradition of the pilgrimage. From early times the pilgrimage was compared to life or the world. Dom Jean Leclercq sees it as a

7. On these pilgrims' customs and manners, see Prescott, pp. 141–42; Heath, pp. 25, 107–125; Sumption, ch. 14 and passim. On Canterbury pilgrims, H. Snowden Ward, *The Canterbury Pilgrimages* (Philadelphia: J. B. Lippincott, 1905) and Francis Watt, *Canterbury Pilgrims and Their Ways* (London: Methuen, 1917). On the holy water of St. Thomas, Sumption, p. 83; J. J. Jusserand, *English Wayfaring Life in the Middle Ages (XIVth Century),* trans. Lucy Toulmin Smith (London, 1890), p. 338, reports that the ampules were stamped with the motto "Optimus egrorum medicus fit Thomas bonorum." A study too recent to be used here is Howard Loxton, *Pilgrimage to Canterbury* (Newton Abbot: David and Charles, 1978).

8. J. J. Bagley and P. B. Rowley, eds., *A Documentary History of England,* vol. 1 (Baltimore: Penguin Books, 1966), p. 216; italics mine. For the arguments against pilgrimages especially by monks and nuns, see Giles Constable, "Opposition to Pilgrimage in the Middle Ages," *Studia Gratiana* 19 (1976): 123–146.

"speculum" of the monastic ideal: monasticism developed two forms of Christian heroism, the solitary life and the active life of preaching; in the same way, the pilgrimage could be a retreat from life or a missionary enterprise.[9] Any pilgrimage was a symbolical journey to the Heavenly Jerusalem but of necessity a real, physical journey too; hence from early times the temptation of *curiositas* was warned against. Curiosity was, as Christian K. Zacher has shown, an essential ingredient of the experience, one that led directly into the impulses behind Renaissance humanism and the Renaissance voyages of exploration.[10]

So it is not surprising that writers wrote books about such a popular institution. More—many more —were written about the pilgrimage than about comparable medieval institutions. A religious and moral element is present in most such writings, sometimes tediously so, sometimes by little more than implication. The most interesting are anecdotal and autobiographical—sometimes, like much travel literature, fanciful—intended for a reader whose pilgrimage is to be vicarious. None that I have found narrates the pilgrimage to Canterbury; if 200,000 pilgrims went each year,[11] it must have been too familiar to deserve

9. "Mönchtum und Peregrinatio in Frühmittelalter," *Römische Quartelschrift für christliche Altertumskunde und Kirchengeschichte* 55 (1960): 212–225, and "Monachisme et pérégrination du IXe au XIIe siècle," *Studia Monastica* 3 (1961): 33–52. For a broader perspective, see Giles Constable, "Monachisme et pèlerinage au Moyen Age," *Revue Historique* 258 (1977): 3–27.

10. Christian K. Zacher, *Curiosity and Pilgrimage: The Literature of Discovery in Fourteenth-Century England* (Baltimore: Johns Hopkins University Press, 1976).

11. Heath, p. 21, reports this figure.

written accounts and the route too easily followed to require an itinerary. There is a small amount of literature pertaining to Compostella and Rome (the two other great medieval pilgrimages) and scattered documents pertaining to lesser shrines. But of the Jerusalem pilgrimage there is a vast literature— between 1100 and 1500 some 526 accounts were written that have survived,[12] and doubtless many more that have not. In the age before the printed book most of these would have been circulated locally—at any given time a reader, even a scholar, would have known only a handful.

But taken together, and surveyed as we can now survey them, they are a significant genre of medieval literature—a neglected genre whose best exemplars deserve better acquaintance. About related genres I will try to hold my tongue. There was a whole other kind of travel book that described voyages into India or the Orient, written by Christian missionaries or merchant-explorers like Marco Polo; later, the accounts of overseas explorers like Columbus or Vespucci.[13] There were pilgrims' songs and a few narra-

---

12. Reinhold Röhricht, *Bibliotheca Geographica Palaestinae: Chronologisches Verzeichnis der von 333 bis 1878 verfassten Literatur über das Heilige Land . . .* (Berlin, 1890); rev. David H. K. Amiran (Jerusalem: Universitas Booksellers, 1963). For other accounts, see Aziz S. Atiya, *The Crusade in the Later Middle Ages* (London: Methuen, 1938), pp. 490–509.

13. On the larger subject of medieval travel, Arthur Percival Newton ed., *Travel and Travellers in the Middle Ages* (London: Kegan Paul, 1926); on travel in England, Jusserand, *English Wayfaring Life*. Edward G. Cox, *A Reference Guide to the Literature of Travel,* University of Washington Publications in Language and Literature, vols. 9, 10, 12 (Seattle: University of Washington, 1935–49), deals mainly with printed editions done in England.

tions in verse, usually doggerel. There was a literature
of the Crusades, some of which shades into the literature of pilgrimage (as in descriptions of the Holy
Land). And there was a body of literature that owed its
existence to contact with Arabic-speaking culture, a
"matter of Araby."[14] But none of this must detain us.

In the body of writings devoted to the Jerusalem
pilgrimage we can discern the _log_, the _guide_, and the
narration. All these involve descriptions of the Holy
Land, but there are some descriptions that neglect the
journey.

Of logs little needs to be said. They are only
curiosities, some of historical interest. There is a short
log by one Thomas Brygg, an Englishman who later
became mayor of Bordeaux.[15] In 1392 he travelled to
the Holy Land as a companion to a nobleman, Thomas
de Swynburne (the English castellan of Guines, ru-
mored to be an ancestor of the _fin de siècle_ poet), and
kept a concise diary. It is a set of dated entries each
beginning "Item": "Item, in the same place we saw an
elephant, a beast of remarkably great size." (This,
quoted in its entirety, is followed by a slightly more
detailed description of a giraffe.) For the most part the
entries are a list of places and expenses; he affixed a
cross where indulgences were obtained. The account
ends at "Baruth," "where we imposed an end on our
pilgrimages in the Holy Land"—one should note that

14. Dorothee Metlitzki, *The Matter of Araby in Medieval England*
(New Haven: Yale University Press, 1977).

15. "Itinerarium ad Sanctam Sepulchram," MS Cambridge
Caius 449, in P. Riant, ed., *Les Archives de L'Orient Latin,* vol. 2
(1882), pp. 380–388.

a pilgrimage consisted of various individual "pilgrimages" to various shrines, and that its end was imposed when these were over, not when the pilgrims got home. Such logs (there is one of a pilgrimage to Canterbury)[16] tell us something of routes and prices; if they tell us more, if they recount the journey itself or describe things seen or heard, they become narrations and so move in the direction of literature. One such log was kept of the pilgrimage of Nicolò Da Este, an Italian nobleman who in 1413 travelled to the Holy Land with a retinue—among them a doctor, four waiters, a chaplain, a purser, a cook and under-cook, a tailor, a barber, two trumpeters, a page, and a *cancellero* (scribe). The last, Luchino Dal Campo, kept a detailed log in literary Tuscan, with comments on the weather, the sights, the events of the journey, meals, entertainments; we read of orange blossoms falling on an outdoor table as the company dined, a storm at sea that terrified them, a Turkish juggler. The book, edited in the nineteenth century, was condensed by Ezra Pound in *The Cantos* XXIV—a testimony to its literary interest.[17]

Of guides there must have been a large number, for there were few useable maps. There were sea-charts used by mariners prior to the fourteenth century, and a few reasonably accurate land maps or road maps, like

16. Henry Littlehales, ed., *Some Notes on the Road from London to Canterbury in the Middle Ages,* Chaucer Society, ser. 2, vol. 30 (London, 1898).

17. "Viaggo a Gerusalemme . . .," ed. Giovanni Ghinassi, in *Collezione di opere inedite o rare dei primi tre secoli della lingua dell'Emilia* (Torino, 1861). On Pound's use of the book, D. J. Hugen, "Small Birds of Cyprus," *Paideuma* 3 (1974): 229–238.

the "Gough" map now preserved in the Bodleian Library dating from ca. 1350. The large world maps like the *mappa mundi* in Hereford Cathedral were artistic and intellectual exercises, not meant to be practical (the one at Hereford shows Scotland and England as separate islands, a political idea rather than a fact). The traveller needed a list of places with directions and distances, that is, an itinerary, and much other information or advice as well.[18] An English guidebook that might be considered characteristic is the *Information for Pilgrims Unto the Holy Land,* sometimes attributed to one John Moreson and printed ca. 1498 by Wynkyn de Worde.[19] It was reprinted in 1515 as *The Way to the Holy Land,* and again in 1524. It is chiefly drawn from a more elaborate work, *The Itineraries of William Wey.*[20] William Wey was a fellow of Eton College, and there is a record dated 1457 of his permission to go on the 1458 pilgrimage. His work survives in a unique manuscript preserved at the Bodleian Library. It contains a table of money changes, a warning about practical details,

18. See Leo Bagrow, *History of Cartography,* rev. R. A. Skelton (Cambridge, Mass.: Harvard University Press, 1966), pp. 61–73. On itineraries, George B. Parks, *The English Traveler to Italy,* vol. 1 (Stanford, Ca.: Stanford University Press, 1954), pp. 179–185.

19. I use the reprint of the 1498 edition (London: Roxburghe Club, 1824). The work was later edited by E. Gordon Duff (London, 1893). The attribution is that of the British Library catalogue; John Moreson is mentioned in the work (f. cii^v) as a "marchaunt of Venyse."

20. G. Williams, ed., *The Itineraries of William Wey* (London: Roxburghe Club: 1857). R. J. Mitchell, *The Spring Voyage: The Jerusalem Pilgrimage in 1458* (London: Murray, 1964), is an account of this pilgrimage; Wey's narration was one of six written by various members of the group.

some mnemonic verses naming places, a list of motives for going to the Holy Land, two narratives of a Jerusalem pilgrimage (one in English and one in Latin) dated 1458 and 1462, word lists of Greek and Hebrew, answers to questions about relics, lists of places, indulgences and shrines, an itinerary to Compostella, a pilgrims' song with music—in short, it is an omnium-gatherum of pilgrimage information. And —significantly—it was keyed to a map. The *Information for Pilgrims,* its debtor, is much less elaborate. It gives a route from Calais to Rome by land, with alternate routes by sea from Naples, Venice, Castellanova, or Milan; and another route from Dover to Jerusalem by the "Duche waye" (up the Rhine, across Bavaria to the Tyrol, and across the Alps by the Reschen pass).[21] These itineraries move from place to place, serially, giving the number of miles between places. In the Holy Land itself the book lists the "pilgrimages" to be made: the "Vale of Josephat," the "Mount of Olivete," the "Vale of Syloe," Mount Sion, Bethlehem, St. John, Bethany, "Flume Jordan," Nazareth, Damascus, Mount Sinai, and Egypt. It names probably all the sites and shrines any pilgrim cared to see; with many it lists related indulgences. There is elaborate advice about money—a vastly complicated matter. Some seventeen changes were necessary between England and "Surrey" (Syria). Coins were good only where they were known: thus the traveller is warned to "take none englysshe golde with you from Brugys, for ye shal lese it in the

21. Parks, p. 294.

chaunge, and also for the moost parte by the waye they
woll not chaunge it." Rhenish gyldens are especially
recommended and "Kateryns" especially warned
against because "the kateryns of the one lordshyp woll
not goo in the nexte lordshyp." There is a list of trib-
utes to be made in the Holy Land, and other useful
hints—at Joppa the "ass man" gets a Venetian grote
"for corteysye." At the end is a word list giving num-
bers, names of foods, greetings, and key phrases (like
"Thou shalt be paid tomorrow") in "Moreske,"
Greek, and Turkish.

This wealth of good advice in the *Information for
Pilgrims* naturally elicits the curiosity and interest of the
reader. The pilgrim is warned to stay near his companions "for by cause of shrewes." He is told to exact clear
agreements from the ship captain in the presence of the
"Duke" of Venice—to provide meat twice a day, to
stop for fresh provisions, not to stop in any port more
than three days, not to take on cargo except as agreed
(lest it displace the passenger), and so on. All that was
troublesome and perilous in medieval travel (and some
that still is) comes menacingly forth in these suggestions.[22] The pilgrim is warned against the "bloody
flux" caused by melons "and suche colde fruytes" in
the Near East: "for they be not accordynge to our
complexion: and they gendre a blody fluxe. And yf
ony englysshe man catche there that syknesse, it is a
grete merveylle but yf he deye therof." One is of
course warned against drinking the water. One is especially to avoid Famagusta in Cyprus, because the air

22. Ibid., pp. 194–216.

are so corrupt there that "many englysshe
thers also have deyed." One must watch all
fects, such as daggers, when one walks about,
the Saracens will "go talkyng bi you & make
chere; but thei woll stele from you yf they
." One ought to avoid the lowest part of the
ey, which is "ryght evyll & smoulderyng hote and
nkynge"; a good place costs fifty ducats, and one
eds a padlock for the door when one goes on land.
One should bring a supply of his own food; laxatives,
restrictives, spices; cooking utensils, dishes, glass cups;
a cage with half a dozen hens; two barrels of wine and
another of water—and one should keep them locked
up in a chest.

The fascination of such matters for the curious
reader was not lost on the author, but he reveals the
ambivalent attitude of medieval men toward worldly
curiosities. After describing the pilgrimages to be
made in the Holy Land, he adds a narrative in the third
person, giving specific dates and a few names. Most
points of interest are religious, but not all. He tells
what kinds of wine "grow" in different places; he
names the rulers of different countries; he mentions a
temple at Delphos in which Apollo was worshipped
and from which Helen was carried off by Paris. He is
fond of pointing out strong castles, directs the traveller
to the famous Labyrinth, reports extensively on the
climate. All this is *curiositas*—the traveller's interest in
what he sees and the reader's in what he hears. But it is
exactly this "curiosity" that led pilgrims astray and put
the pilgrimage in bad repute. Against curiosity the
Fathers and preachers always warned pilgrims; it was

the natural antithesis in medieval thought to the reli gious conception of pilgrimage.[23] The ideal pilgrin would have travelled, as St. Bernard of Clairvaux is said to have done along the shores of Lake Léman, with his eyes upon the ground to shut out the glories of the world.[24] But few pilgrims travelled so. It was largely the fascination of travel itself that made men go on pilgrimages, that made pilgrimages such a fundamental institution of medieval society and made written accounts of them so interesting to read. Yet that fascination, they knew, was wrong. Hence at the end of the narrative which describes the pilgrimage, after a brief mention of the return route, the *Information for Pilgrims* lapses into Latin and closes with a somber paragraph *De brevitate et vanitate huius mundi*. Here is just the kind of warning medieval men heard all the time— *contemptus mundi* is the name they gave it. The passage is in Latin, and it may well have been added by a later hand; but we must not think it a mere appendage, for it points to the real concerns that lay behind the institution. "Go to the sepulchres of the dead," it warns, "and look upon samples of the living. Their bones are fallen apart, the man himself disappears, yet his cause is reserved until the Judgment. . . . Intent on riches, he increased his fields, planted vineyards, filling his barns in many storerooms, and was happy in his abundance.

23. See Zacher, ch. 2.

24. See Alanus, *S. Bernardi Vita secunda*, 16 (*Patrologia Latina*, ed. J.-P. Migne, 185: 496), who says only that he did not see. John Benton has suggested to me that the pious motive is owing to J. A. Symonds and that in fact Bernard induced a trance-like state against pain while travelling.

And behold now all things are removed from his eyes.
He lies in the tomb returned to dust. That flesh of his
which he nourished on delicacies has disintegrated. . . .
Let the living know the remains of the dead. . . ."

From the eleventh century on, there are many such
guides. They are practical aids for the traveller and
pilgrim: they give an itinerary and name the places to
be seen. In most there is no sense of the author's self,
and no anecdotes or narrative. Here and there a local
legend or a curiosity: crocodiles,[25] or details about the
Templars and Hospitallers,[26] or the two fearsome ser-
pents of Egypt (out of Herodotus III.109).[27] In one
work, we learn that the Georgians came from the land
of Feminie and to this day burn off a girl's right breast
when she is born so that their women can draw a bow
in battle.[28] One author, Johannes Phocas, a Cretan
who made the pilgrimage in 1185, tells us that he is
describing his sojourn in the Holy Land for those who
have not been there, "if it be pleasant to listen to accounts of what it is enjoyable to behold"; but he gives
little more than an itinerary, a list of shrines, and a few
local legends, with no suggestion of an actual pilgrim-

25. As in the work attributed to "Fetullus," "Description of
Jerusalem and the Holy Land" (ca. 1130), trans. J. R. MacPherson,
Library of the Palestine Pilgrims' Text Society 5 (1897). Sub-
sequent references to this series will be cited as LPPTS.

26. As in "Anonymous Pilgrims" (eleventh and twelfth centuries), trans. Aubrey Stewart, LPPTS 6 (1897), no. 5.

27. As in Ernoul (1231), chs. 7–10 of his *Chronicle,* trans. C. R.
Conder, LPPTS 6 (1888).

28. "The City of Jerusalem" (ca. 1187), trans. C. R. Conder,
LPPTS 6 (1888). The Latin text edited by Titus Tobler, *Descrip-
tiones terrae sanctae ex seculo VIII. IX. XII. et XV* (Leipzig, 1874), pp.
197–224.

age told from his own experience.[29] Another author, Theodorich, who made the pilgrimage ca. 1172, makes a similar promise and keeps it better; his work is put together from "what we have seen" and what has been found truthful in the reports of others, and is intended for those who have not made the pilgrimage.[30] What he writes sounds quite like a guide; but he was a keen observer and describes some traveller's details that have no religious value at all—the flat roofs of houses in Jerusalem, for example, in which people catch rain water. In the fourteenth and fifteenth centuries such guides are little changed; three have maps,[31] which make them more specific and useful, and at least two authors emphasize what they saw themselves with their own eyes, though they saw little that others had not seen before.[32]

29. His work was translated into Latin by one Leo Allatius with a brief preface, and into English by Aubrey Stewart, LPPTS 5 (1889).

30. "Description of the Holy Places," trans. Aubrey Stewart, LPPTS 5 (1891); he is probably the Theodorich who became Bishop of Würzburg in 1223.

31. Apart from William Wey's (see n. 20 above), Marino Sanuto, "Secrets for True Crusaders to Help Them Recover the Holy Land" (1321), trans. Stewart, LPPTS 12 (1886), includes maps of Jerusalem, the Near East, and the Holy Land. John Poloner, "Description of the Holy Land" (1421), trans. Aubrey Stewart, LPPTS 6 (1894), gives a map of the Holy Land marked in squares for reference.

32. Poloner, and "Odoricus de Foro Julii," *De terra sancta* (ca. 1320), in J. C. M. Laurent, ed., *Peregrinatores medii aevi quatuor* (Leipzig, 1864). (This is "pseudo–Odoric," not to be confused with Odoric of Pordenone, d. 1331; the latter travelled into the Orient and his account, dictated in 1330, was one of Mandeville's chief sources.)

There were, though, always keen observers and sightseers; and so there were always some accounts of travels that went beyond the function of guidebooks into the fascination of travel itself. As early as 1102–03 (we have the date on internal evidence) an English traveller named Saewulf went into the Holy Land and wrote down his experiences.[33] His report is perhaps the only real pilgrimage account written by an Englishman until the fifteenth century. William of Malmesbury mentions a merchant of that name and time who in old age entered the abbey of Malmesbury.[34] Saewulf reports things heard as well as seen, uses "I" and "we," and adopts a stylized conversational manner with phrases like "what more should I say?" He tells an anecdote or two about the dangers of the journey, and is as interested in classical as in biblical antiquity; his story (or the manuscript) breaks off after his description of the Holy Land as he approaches Constantinople on the return journey. He tells about the Colossus at Rhodes; describes a storm at sea, which he observed from a beach; tells how twenty-six Saracen ships menaced the pilgrims' ships but fled when they found them armed. He adds with satisfaction that "our people from Joppa afterwards captured three of those same ships and enriched themselves with their spoil."

In 1232 and again about 1280, one Brocardus (or Burchardus) of Mt. Sion, a Dominican priest from

33. "Pilgrimage to Jerusalem and the Holy Land," trans. C. Brownlow, LPPTS 4 (1897) with Latin text; also trans. Thomas Wright, *Early Travels in Palestine* (London, 1848). See Parks, p. 151.

34. *De gestis pontificum Anglorum,* IV. 146.

Strassburg or Magdeburg, travelled in the Holy Land. In his account, said to be influential on later works, he claims to set down nothing he had not seen with his own eyes, at least at a distance.[35] He describes terrains and cities more extensively than others had done, and he uses a map-like system of dividing land into quarters and those quarters into thirds ("like the twelve winds of heaven"), with Jerusalem, of course, in the center. He is as interesting a personality as Saewulf, with the same eye for captivating sights; he describes in detail an irrigation system in Tyre; gives a lush account of "apples of paradise" (bananas); describes noblewomen's eunuchs; and tells about the "Latins" in the Holy Land, "our own people," who came as penitents or fugitives and remained as an enclave of outlaws.

Such was the state of pilgrimage literature when Marco Polo travelled to the Orient and returned to write while in prison (1298–99) the great account of his travels. The work—like other tales of travel into the Orient, those of Carpini (who made his journey in 1245), Roubrouquis (1253), and Odoric of Pordenone (1320)—is not pertinent to our purposes, for it was by no means the story of a pilgrimage; but it has in common with the more promising strain of pilgrimage narratives its curiosity about distant places and strange customs, its personal and autobiographical manner, and the fact that it tells a story for the reader's delight. Polo's collaborator, Rustichello of Pisa, was a romance writer, and his hand has been clearly demonstrated in

35. "Descriptio terrae sanctae," trans. Aubrey Stewart, LPPTS 12 (1896); also in Laurent, ed.

set descriptions and stock scenes like those in his other works.[36] The book, as no reader can fail to remember, is full of exotic wonders. Perhaps it shows that truth is stranger than fiction, though it is hard not to suspect some amount of embroidery even in supposed eyewitness accounts. In addition, its author included many a tale he had heard, of dog-faced men, or male and female islands, or "Prester John," without vouching for their accuracy: they were narratives within a narrative and he could retell them with detachment. He and his collaborator, in their prologue, are quite explicit on the point: "Our book will relate [wonders and curiosities] to you plainly in due order, as they were related by Messer Marco Polo, a wise and noble citizen of Venice, who has seen them with his own eyes. There is also much here that he has not seen but has heard from men of credit and veracity. We will set down things heard as heard, so that our book may be an accurate record, free from any sort of fabrication." Many a pilgrim author made a similar claim.

The fourteenth century begins the great age of pilgrimage narratives. One of the most remarkable and readable is the *Itinerarium* of Wilhelm von Boldensele, a German Dominican who travelled to the Holy Land in 1332–33 and completed his book in 1337.[37] It is the

36. See *The Travels of Marco Polo,* trans. and ed. Ronald Latham (Baltimore: Penguin Books, 1958), pp. 17–18. The discovery of Rustichello's (or Rusticiano's) contribution was made by L. F. Benedetto; its importance is slighted by Leonardo Olschki, *Marco Polo's Asia,* trans. John A. Scott (Berkeley and Los Angeles: University of California Press, 1960), pp. 48–51, 129, 354–355.

37. Edited by C. L. Grotefend in *Die Edelherren von Boldensele oder Boldensen* (Hannover, 1855).

chief source of the first half of *Mandeville's Travels*. It is not a personal or autobiographical account—he uses "I" as an objective observer, not a participant in the action, says nothing of his fellow pilgrims, and recounts few personal anecdotes. All the same, one gets a lively sense of his zestful curiosity, his powers of observation, and his active mind. He is capable of apostrophizing and meditating on, for example, ruins; and, like any German tourist, he cannot help exclaiming over things. "Ach!" he cries on seeing the Dead Sea, "that such a holy and delightful river should be mixed into such a detestable body of water." As he gets into the Holy Land there is more detail about biblical places, to be sure, but his route went from Syria and Egypt through the Holy Land to Damascus, so he is able to tell of pyramids, slaves, camels, giraffes; he is interested in the terrain, the wine, the food. He tells of seeing three live elephants: "Now the elephant is a very large animal having a tough skin after the manner of fishes' scales; very easily disciplined . . ." and so on with details about their tusks, teeth, trunk, and manner of eating; those he saw had been trained to bow and touch their heads to earth, which he explains is the way of honoring guests in that country. Like other travellers he exclaims over bananas ("an elongated fruit, called the apple of paradise, having a wonderful taste, and soft, so that it melts easily in the mouth"), which he laments are too perishable to take home, and adds the common bit of information that if you cut them crosswise you can see a crucifix. He tells us, of course, about religious places he visited; at one point, describing a monastery, he cannot resist telling what the monks ate.

A similar work, by another German, is that of Ludolf von Suchem, who made the journey to Jerusalem in 1336–41.[38] He tells us that he writes entirely from memory and includes tales he heard as well as what he saw: "Let no one suppose that I beheld with my eyes each several one of the things which I intend to put in this book," for he has taken some matters from "ancient books of history" and some "from the lips of truthful men"—and would have put in more but for "ignorant cavillers and scoffers." He describes the perils of the sea, tells of the places he saw, and includes a fair number of anecdotes. He uses an authorial "I" throughout. He is interested in strange sights, riches, and prices. And he is interested in history. We get from him, too, bits of strange lore—the flying fish bred from the seeds of a fruit tree, or the wine-colored balsam with curative powers (which may be found in *Mandeville's Travels,* ch. 5)—along with wonders, by now routine, like crocodiles and camels.

Such accounts inevitably reveal an interest in the beliefs of infidels; and it is remarkable in the age of Crusades and Inquisitions to find sometimes a calm and disinterested tolerance. Ricoldus de Monte Crucis (to give his name in Latin), a Dominican from Florence who died in 1309, was chiefly interested in what people believed—the Turks, the Tartars, the Baldacs, Jaco-

38. "Description of the Holy Land," trans. Aubrey Stewart, LPPTS 12 (1895); it was written in 1350.

bites, Maronites, Nestorines, and Saracens.[39] He reports their customs, attitudes, and doctrines with
interest and detachment, though he is not averse to
pointing out their "errors." He can see much good in
Saracens, for example—they are prayerful, have the
habit of cleanliness, give alms to the poor, revere God's
name, are grave in their manners and kind to foreigners, and show brotherly love to one another. He then
excoriates their *law:* it is *confusa, occulta, mendacissima,
irracionabilis,* and *violenta,* and he devotes a chapter to
each of these points, denigrating their claims to
prophecies and miracles. But perhaps the good in the
men themselves, despite the shortcomings of their
law, would have given a Christian reader pause. This
possible implication was drawn out by Brocardus.[40]
Having told of the Latins—"our own people"—who
live in the Holy Land as outlaws, he describes the
Mohammedan religion with great tolerance, respectfully and, I think, accurately. He then turns to various
Christian peoples, who come off the worse by comparison. He speaks respectfully and objectively of the
Armenians, and of the Nestorians, who are not here-
tics, as their name implies, but men of a simple and
devout life: "Yet I do not deny that there may be fools
among them, seeing that even the Church of Rome
itself is not free from fools."

Such detachment, which brushes the edge of irony,
deserves comparison with another fourteenth-century
work, this one by an armchair traveller, Francesco Pet-
rarca. Petrarch's work, the *Itinerarium Siriacum,* about

39. *Liber peregrinationis,* in Laurent, ed., pp. 103–141.
40. LPPTS 12, p. 107.

6,000 words long, was written probably in the late 1350s or early 1360s.[41] Petrarch says he wrote it at the request of a Milanese nobleman who intended to make the Jerusalem pilgrimage (the humanist himself had declined to join the company for various reasons, especially his fear of the sea). Asked to report on the things one should see, he divides the objects of a traveller's intentions among religion, knowledge, and history (*memoria exemplorum*). He begins the work by warning that Fortune rarely lets things turn out as planned, and reminds the reader that "we know many things we have not seen and are ignorant of many things we see." His implicit advice was to see Italy first: he spends more than half the work mentioning places in Italy and Sicily, selecting them for their significance in ancient history or classical literature—he mentions Vergil often. His bookishness shapes his remarks on Asia Minor too. He leads the traveller through the Holy Land and then into Egypt and other Old Testament places, as was often the practice; but he cannot, for example, resist mentioning Alexander, Julius Caesar, and Mark Antony in connection with Egypt. His projected itinerary may be the first instance of a literary and historical pilgrimage. He closes by sending his reader off on his journey and himself back to his studies: with a true Petrarchan twist he allows that the pilgrims will end up being more learned and more holy than he.

It is a temptation to linger over the fifteenth-century accounts of pilgrimages, for they are the most fun

41. Edited with an introduction by Giacomo Lumbroso in *Atti della Reale Accademia dei Lincei,* serie quarta, vol. 4 (Rome, 1888), pp. 390–403.

to read. Their authors are unabashedly autobiographical—devoted sightseers and great note-takers.
The names and deeds of their fellow pilgrims begin to
play a part, and the curiosities and excitements of
foreign travel come to the fore. They are writing, they
sometimes tell us, for future travellers or Crusaders;
and indeed it is hard to imagine any reader of such
works not wanting to go East himself. They abound
with details of caravans, sandstorms, Damascus
blades, Turkish baths, Near Eastern horses, slaves,
caviar, olive oil ("only fit for Greeks"), the cakes that
Turkish women bake, and such quotidian matters as
the packing of camels, prices, guides. One writer, Bertrandon de la Brocquiere, a counselor to the Duke of
Burgundy who made his pilgrimage in the 1430s, was
especially fascinated by "The Turk," observing carefully the horsemen and slaves of this potentate (he
found him at the age of thirty already very fat).[42]

I suppose I should mention here another book dating from about the 1430s, *The Book of Margery Kempe*.
It is often reckoned the first autobiography in English;
and, as it happens, Dame Margery was (like the Wife of
Bath) a married woman who left her husband behind
and went on all the major pilgrimages—like the Wife
she had been to Jerusalem, Rome, and St. James of
Compostella; in addition, to Germany; and she had hit
the major English shrines. But her book, dictated to a
priest (it refers to her throughout as "this creature")
is not about her pilgrimages. It is about her. For she
was quite mad—an incurable hysteric with a large

42. "Travels," in Wright, pp. 283–382.

paranoid trend. To the medieval way of thinking this was not incompatible with real visions,[43] but to the modern reader she is less interesting as a mystic than as a case history. The chapters of her book devoted to her pilgrimages only tell about her seeing visions and hearing voices, her incessant weeping (she would weep and cry "It is full merry in heaven" when others laughed), and, starting in Jerusalem, her uncontrollable screaming. She did not overlook people's reactions: she spoiled her fellow pilgrims' fun and was the object of much hostility and some pity, plus a fair amount of awe, for she may after all have been the real thing, a holy madwoman. There is not in her book a scintilla of traveller's curiosity, so we get no bananas, giraffes, or elephants from Margery; not even descriptions of the shrines. We can say that as a writer (or raconteur) she was gifted, but she offers little that is useful to our purposes; one would much prefer an account dictated by the Wife of Bath.

The most famous pilgrimage of the century was that of 1483–84. One of its members, Bernhard von Breydenbach, the dean of Mainz cathedral, set out to write a guide; his work, very widely known, includes six remarkable view-maps of cities (the originals done by an artist he brought with him) handsomely colored on long, fold-out sheets.[44] Among them is Venice,

43. See Penelope B. R. Doob, *Nebuchadnezzar's Children: Conventions of Madness in Middle English Literature* (New Haven and London: Yale University Press, 1974), pp. 31–33, and *The Book of Margery Kempe,* ed. Sanford Brown Meech and Hope Emily Allen, Early English Text Society, o.s. 212 (1940), pp. lxiv–lxvi.

44. *Peregrinatio in terram sanctam* (Moguntina, 1486; Speyer, 1490 and 1502). See Hugh W. Davies, *Bernhard von Breydenback and His*

looking not very different from the way it looks today.
He lists shrines, gives the reader a sample contract with
a ship captain, and ends with tips on seasickness and
delousing. He includes word lists and transcribes the
Arabic alphabet (his is thought the first European book
to do so) with other alphabets as well.[45] In his introduction he begs the reader to overlook it if the human
temptation of irrelevant curiosity has overtaken him,
and this the reader can do easily: his sober, useful book
is peppered with details of interest—five pages of il-
lustrations showing Eastern costumes, another showing animals; an account of an altercation among the
camel-drivers; descriptions of a strange animal seen in
Egypt called a "coppin," of an eclipse of the moon, of
egg incubators (a great marvel); an account of Mohammedan errors; and an anecdote of how in Cairo
he and his fellow pilgrims—about 150 in all—were
mistaken for slaves and their guide offered ten ducats a
head for them.

   With him in this large group were a Franciscan and a
Dominican friar, Paul Walther and Felix Fabri, who
both wrote accounts of their adventures. Brother Paul,
heavy with rhetoric and brooding by temperament,
can never forget he is a churchman; but his anecdotes
are often personal all the same—he closes, for exam-

Journey to the Holy Land, 1483–4: A Bibliography (London: J. and J.
Leighton, 1911). Apart from the three Latin editions, there were
three in German, three in French, and one each in Flemish and
Spanish.

   45. Hebrew, Chaldaic, Jacobite, Ethiopian, and Greek; in the
first German edition and the Spanish edition there is an Armenian
alphabet.

ple, by telling how he said mass in Venice when it was under interdict, was declared irregular, and had to get absolution from Cardinal Juliano, protector of his order.[46] He was given to quarrels, worries, and fretful prayers, and for this reason some modern commentators dismiss him with impatience; the more "objective" pilgrim writers are the more admired. Yet for all his self-concern his book has interest as a piece of autobiographical writing, and as a historical document that reveals scruples, guilt, and deep joyous feelings grounded in religion. Intellect, too: he was interested in the history of the places he visited, and a devoted fact finder. And he was not without interest in others: he tells feelingly and in detail of hearing laymen's confessions, exclaims over the spiritual state of apostates. When *he* describes an elephant, his amazement jumps off the page ("I say with certainty this animal seemed to me more remarkable than all the beasts of the earth, for I can scarcely describe with my pen the form and disposition of his body. . . . He held his head down like a pig, had small eyes like a pig. . . . He did everything with his nose. . . . He ate grain, and he lifted the grain with his nose and curling it about put it in his mouth. And this animal is smart, for he took a lot of water into his nose, and raised it, and held it out, and sprayed the water all over the people—he was making a joke"). He must have taken notes, for he gives a day-by-day account, in the past tense, with dates and places; in this respect he is *too* circumstantial—there's too much rep-

46. Paul Walther, *Itinerarium in terram sanctam . . . ,* ed. M. Sollweck, in *Bibliothek des litterarischen Vereins in Stuttgart,* vol. 192 (Tübingen, 1892).

etition about getting fed, packing camels, and such. He tells how the Christian wife of his dragoman longed to hear mass (he obliged her) and wished aloud that she lived "in partibus fidelium"—to which he adds, with a Crusader's spirit, "Would that it were so!" At one point he pauses to take stock of his experience, systematically after the German fashion. He has done three kinds of exercise, he says. First, the physical labor required; second, exercises both physical and spiritual, like collecting materials for a treatise on the genealogy of Christ from Adam on down, and for a treatise on the life and doctrine of Mohammed, and of course like visiting the holy places; third, exercises entirely spiritual. It deserves to be added that he was about sixty-one when he made his journey.

Brother Felix was younger—about forty-two—when he joined the pilgrimage, and he had been on the Jerusalem pilgrimage once before in 1480.[47] He returned from his second voyage to write the longest, most circumstantial, and most modern of all pilgrimage accounts. He is the Proust of the genre. Like Proust he began with an overture: a brief description of his earlier pilgrimage. It had been a shambles. His group had trouble finding a ship captain to take them because of danger from the Turks, and when they got to Jerusalem they were rushed through the round of holy

47. Felix Fabri, *Evagatorium in Terrae Sanctae, Arabiae, et Egypti Peregrinationem,* ed. C. D. Hassler, in ibid., vols. 2–4 (1843–49). "The Wanderings of Felix Fabri," trans. Aubrey Stewart, LPPTS 7–10, 2 vols. (London, 1893), runs to some 1,300 pages, yet omits sections, among them the whole journey home after the pilgrimage to Sinai. Passages quoted are from this translation.

places in a mere nine days. Brother Felix wanted to stay on, but he could find no companions who spoke German or Latin (oddly, he seems never to have made any effort to learn other languages, even Italian). So he vowed to return: "I determined and vowed that I would return as speedily as possible, and I regarded this pilgrimage as merely the preamble to that which I intended to make. As a student who means to commit some passage to memory first reads it over carelessly, and then reads it again slowly and leisurely, taking sufficient time to impress it on his mind, so I did with regard to my determination; and I was far from being satisfied with what I saw, nor did I commit the things which I saw to memory, but kept them for a future pilgrimage." Later, the holy places he had visited seemed to him "shrouded in a dark mist, as though I had beheld them in a dream; and I seemed to myself to know less about all the holy places than I did before I visited them, whence it happened that when I was questioned about the holy places I could give no distinct answers, nor could I write a clear description of my journey." But this first journey got fear and confusion out of his system. His overture describing it focuses on its terrors—a miraculous deliverance from a storm, and again a near shipwreck during which he had dreadful fantasies of things he had heard, of lifeboats overloaded where "those who see the danger of those in the boats cut off with their swords the fingers and hands of men who are hanging to the oars or to the ship's side meaning to get into the boats."

The overture is really a reverse image, for Brother Felix approached his second journey with resolve and joy and came to it prepared. And he approached it as a writer: he promised his brothers in his convent that he would write a narrative of his travels, a "grave" narrative in which he would "often mix fun and amusement with serious matters." He read everything he could get his hands on—accounts by pilgrims and Crusaders, and descriptions of the Holy Land. And he wrestled with his motives, asking himself whether he was tempted by the devil or "guilty of the sin of idle curiosity, or moved by frivolity." When the time came, in 1483— and in April—it came as an invitation from a nobleman to join a large party as its chaplain (he had already, on the quiet, attained written permission from the Master of his order).

So he had a plan. He took notes voluminously—at night, he says, or aboard ship during the day, even sometimes when riding on a camel or an ass. To the extent that his book reflects what he wrote *en route* it contains the vestiges of a log, and there are dissertations on all kinds of practical matters that give it the quality of a guide. But it is a narration—a *book,* I want to say—which he entitled *Evagatorium* ("wanderings"), not without irony, for he was incapable of omitting anything: his book compares with Proust's in length too. Before he got to Venice, at Treviso, he planned to omit detailed descriptions of places until he got to the Holy Land, saving them for the return journey. This was a remarkable innovation, one that gives a spectral quality to the events of the journey out, makes the descriptions of the Holy Places dazzling by contrast, keeps the focus on religion, and inspires curiosity about the journey home.

Friar Felix Fabri was a born storyteller and, I am sure, a compulsive writer. He writes in workaday Latin, knowing he will be sneered at by "those priests who neglect the Gospels and prophets to read Vergil and the Latin poets and rhetoricians." But of course he was of the Order of Preachers and had rhetoric—*pulpit* rhetoric—at his fingertips. His plain style is a speaker's style, and it is powerful for its abundance of detail, its candor, and for his timing, wit, intellect. His very considerable learning is medieval learning—he cites authors like Aristotle, or Isidore of Seville, Thomas Aquinas, Albertus Magnus, Boccaccio's scholarly works. He had such classical learning as a medieval man possessed at second hand—I see no evidence that he knew Greek or that he had read the ancient Latin poets to any extent. But his insights are often surprisingly modern: "As a bird cannot fly without its feathers and wings," he tells us, "even so a ship of the greatest burthen cannot move without sails, which are its wings and feathers. So when the poets speak of winged horses, they merely mean ships, as, for instance, Perseus came from Greece on a winged horse, and saved Andromeda from the rock at Joppa, etc."

His notion of a book is modern too. Though the printing press had only just been invented during his lifetime, his spun-out tale seems intended for a modern kind of reader who can skip and skim. He does go on so! But he is a master at whetting our curiosity about what is to come. Like garrulous writers of the better kind he is solicitous of his reader. For example, at Venice, during a delay, he persuaded his companions that they should each day make a pilgrimage to a local

church; he describes church after church until it begins
to seem as if they are all the same (an experience familiar still to sojourners in Venice), then disarmingly tells
us, when the ship is ready to sail, "we were tired of
Venice." During one of his long digressions he even
tells us "I am weary of writing." Bored as we are
bored, he recaptures in an almost Conradian fashion
the tedium, the *travail,* of medieval travel. And so he
makes the reader experience the sight of the Holy Land
from aboard ship with the excitement and relief the
pilgrims themselves felt, weeping as they sang *Te
Deum* at the top of their lungs (later, approaching
Jerusalem, they sang *Te Deum* too, but softly now so as
not to anger their Saracen escort). Other pilgrimage
accounts kept the journey interesting with bananas and
giraffes; Brother Felix, saving material for the return
journey, makes us feel the anxiety and suspense, and so
I believe makes us feel the emotions of the medieval
pilgrimage, emotions strange to us, of the kind
Huizinga has helped us understand. One of these was
longing:

. . . I used to stand at the prow in the early twilight, hoping
to see the Holy Land before the sun arose; and I used to greet
the rising sun with joy, because without his help I could not
see that land. But when I saw the sun risen high above the
sea, with no land shown at his rising, I sadly turned away,
and for a time busied myself with other matters. Thus was it
also with other pilgrims, not, indeed, with all, but only
those who loved and longed for the Holy Land. *Ach, mein
Gott!* how sweet the love of a heavenly country can be to the
devout and contemplative, when undevout, wretched, sinful, wandering pilgrims feel so pleasant, so deep, and so keen

a longing for an earthly one! Even as Mary Magdalen, burning with the fire of love, often bowed herself down and looked into the sepulchre where her Beloved lay, so doth the loving pilgrim often rise up in his ship and gaze fixedly toward the east, that he may behold the land wherein is the sepulchre of his Beloved.

Another pilgrims' emotion was *joy*. Their joy on arriving was close to hysteria. Some pilgrims threw away their shoes that they might walk barefoot in the Holy City. At the Holy Sepulchre they knelt down and kissed the earth that the Lord had walked on. And here Brother Felix in a rare moment addresses the reader directly—

O my brother! hadst thou been with me in that court at that hour, thou wouldst have seen such plenteous tears, such bitter heartfelt groans, such sweet wailings, such deep sighs, such true sorrow, such sobs from the inmost breast, such peaceful and gladsome silence, that hadst thou a heart of stone it must have melted, and thou wouldst have burst into a flood of tears together with the weeping pilgrims. I saw there some pilgrims lying powerless on the ground, forsaken by their strength, and as it were forgetful of their own being by reason of their excessive feeling of devotion. Others I saw who wandered hither and thither from one corner to another, beating their breasts, as though they were driven by an evil spirit. Some knelt on the earth with their bare knees, and prayed with tears, holding their arms out in the form of a cross . . .

—and so on describing various kinds of behavior, including that of "some dull and unprofitable pilgrims, nay rather brute beasts" who just stood and laughed mockingly at these excesses.

But it shows something about Felix Fabri's extraordinary mind that as he reaches a climactic scene, the ascent of a high mountain from which they could see all the terrain of the Holy Land magnificently spread before them, he pauses to call into question all the emotions spurred by seeing the holy places, to remind his reader that true devotion is in the heart, and to claim with not much show of humility that he could raise more devotion by speaking:

Good and simple Christians believe that if they were at the places where the Lord Jesus wrought the work of our redemption, they would derive much devotion from them; but I say to these men of a truth that meditation about these places, and listening to descriptions of them, is more efficacious than the actual seeing and kissing of them. Unless a pilgrim hath before his eyes some living example of devotion, the place helps him little in the matter of true holiness. Those weepings and sobbings which are common at the holy places arise for the most part from the fact that when one pilgrim weeps another cannot refrain from tears, and so sometimes all of them lament together; or because some people have the art of working themselves up to weep even in matters unconnected with religion. Such people as these shed many futile tears at the holy places, and make a howling at almost all of them, not because of the power which the place exercises over them, albeit the places do certainly tend to devotion, but because of the ease with which they weep. But I have no doubt of this, that were there ten good Christians in my cell at Ulm, who had a desire to see the Holy Land and the places sacred to the Lord Jesus, I could rouse their devotion and stir up their souls more deeply by my talk about those places than if they were actually lying bowed to the earth in the holy places themselves.

Eight years after Brother Felix's return, probably while he was still writing, Columbus set sail. In 1484, the year he returned from his pilgrimage, Columbus was already in Portugal promoting his enterprise. That voyage was to change geography and to change travel literature too. Felix Fabri in his cell at Ulm did not know it was the end of an era.

It is hard to stifle enthusiasm for this long, long book. The modern penchant is to cut, to express impatience at what seems, while one is reading it, long-winded and "self-indulgent." But after we are through reading, we remember the promontories of our interest, forget what we skimmed: we can still warm to "sprawl," and the sprawling writer who succeeds wins more admiration for the sheer magnitude of his endeavor than the most artful sonneteer. Brother Felix's book covers everything and covers it in more detail than anyone else had. Coming at the end of a tradition of writing, he produces its ultimate exemplar by sheer inclusiveness. Nowhere can one read a fuller description of the sights to see in the Holy Land. But he goes beyond this task: he tells all about everything in the experience itself—gives us little treatises, as they actually are, or essays, on galley slaves, the perils of the sea (in three parts), life aboard ship, the indignities suffered at the hands of Saracens, sandstorms, sickness, the lack of water, quarrels among the pilgrims. He gives, too, a history of Jerusalem ending with its conquest by the Western nations. And homey details—the old women who travelled with them and had more endurance than the men, a workman who repaired the rudder of their ship ("but how that workman could breathe under water, and how he could strike with his hammer there, and how he could remain so long in the salt water, I cannot understand. But this much I know, that the human mind has dominion over fire and water, even as the stars have dominion over the human mind"). The strange passion for theft, especially petty theft, that overtakes people aboard ship gets its share of attention (if one puts his pen down it is gone, and how hard to replace it aboard ship); or how he missed his convent, or (while swimming in the Jordan) his friar's habit.

He is one of the greatest writers of his century, and his book is one of the great books of the Middle Ages, yet it is almost completely unknown.

Most important, he gives—so far as I know for the first time in such writings—a detailed, a *rendered* account of the homecoming. He tells how the pilgrimage was declared complete at Jerusalem, how his German companions departed for Venice (pirates, storms) and all arrived safe, how many others died, how he alone of his group stayed behind in Jerusalem as he planned. "Praise be to God!" he writes, "here endeth the pilgrimage which we made together to Jerusalem." Then turn the page and you find the beginning of his pilgrimage to Mt. Sinai, hundreds of pages long. And so the indefatigable friar gives us, as he promised, a detailed description of places on the way home. He tells of the inn at Venice to which he returned, of meeting some of his countrymen there, and of the journey back across the Alps to his convent at Ulm. It is the first homecoming scene in pilgrimage literature: his brothers are at their prayers and no one knows he is back from his odyssey until the monastery dog recognizes his step and greets him with fervent barking. It is touching after the fashion of modern (and ancient) endings, for the emphasis now is upon the experience of travel itself, and a part of that is arriving home. With this innovation we have come to the close of the Middle Ages.

Until Friar Felix's book, no account of a pilgrimage that I have seen gives equal weight to the return journey; most writers barely mention it, and some do not do that. The same is true of "voyages": Friar Odoric of Pordenone, Friar William of Roubrouquis, and Marco Polo made no mention of the return journey, and Carpini accorded it one short chapter in which he mentions no place closer to home than Bohemia. Simone Sigoli, who made his pilgrimage exactly a hundred years earlier than Friar Felix, wrote a fairly circumstantial day-by-day account, with personal details (like his upset stomach), and he *does* recount the journey home place by place—but he doesn't make a dramatic scene of the homecoming.[48] In the fifteenth century, as in the *Information for Pilgrims,* authors sometimes tell briefly what route they took home. Bernhard von Breydenbach, one of Friar Felix's fellow pilgrims, describes the return of his party from Alexandria, but only as far as Venice: some twenty-five of the fifty pilgrims in his party, we know, dropped out at Jerusalem, while the rest contracted to go on to the Dead Sea or into Egypt. At Venice, they dispersed for their different nations. For some, there *was* no return. On the Jerusalem pilgrimage there were almost always some deaths; it was

48. "Viaggio al Monte Sinai," ed. Carlo Gargiolli, *Viaggi in Terra Santa* (Firenze, 1862), pp. 133–268.

indeed considered desirable to die in Jerusalem.[49] And pilgrims were constantly waylaid because of sickness. The return voyage was a mere contingency, an anticlimax.

The climax of the Jerusalem pilgrimage was the Holy Land. There, the groups made a series of "pilgrimages" to all the appropriate shrines, including usually the very desirable excursion to the river Jordan. A further voyage to Egypt or elsewhere was optional, not part of the format. When everything in Jerusalem had been seen, the pilgrimage was declared complete.[50] The pilgrims' experience of Jerusalem took the form of a drama or an allegory of the life of Christ, an idea that survives in the liturgical practice of the Catholic Church, the Stations (or "Way") of the Cross.[51] While there are descriptions of the Holy Land that say nothing about the getting there at all, in general authors described the voyage *to* the destination in detail and finished with a detailed description of the experience in the Holy Land. In this we have a real difference between the medieval mind and the modern. For us the homecoming, the recognition scene, the sweet relief of getting back, lessons learned and memories nurtured—all are part of our idea of travel. When we come to the end of those fat volumes written by Friar Felix Fabri and read of his touching arrival at his convent in Ulm, the dog sniffing and barking to welcome him, his brothers rushing to him from their devotions, we feel at last in familiar country. It seems

49. Sumption, pp. 130–132.
50. See Prescott, ch. 8.
51. Sumption, p. 93.

astonishing that until then no writer had seen the possibilities immanent in the thrill of return. I think the medievals did feel such a thrill: they gave us our English word for it, *homecoming,* and described the experience in romances. But homecoming did not fit the idea of pilgrimage.

The idea of pilgrimage, and the institution, go back to the wandering and ascetic homelessness of early Christian times, and these practices positively discouraged a return. The hermits and desert fathers of the primitive church travelled into the wilderness to stay sequestered from civilization; they called the experience an exile.[52] Some doubtless returned home, but the return was never part of the venture. Nor was a destination: they were practicing a form of spiritual recklessness, a search of the spirit in which the only destination would be union with God and eternal life. This tradition of aimless wandering continued throughout the Middle Ages in various forms—in the place-to-place travels of the *Gyrovagi* and *Circumcelliones,* in the voyages of Irish missionaries, in "knight errancy."

52. See Hans Frhr. von Campenhausen, *Die asketische Heimatlosigkeit im altkirchlichen und frühmittelalterlichen Mönchtum,* Sammlung gemeinverständlicher Vorträge und Schriften aus dem Gebiet der Theologie und Religionsgeschichte, no. 149 (Tübingen, 1930). On the development of the pilgrimage from this early ascetic homelessness, see the articles by Leclercq cited earlier, and Zacher, ch. 3, who collects a number of scriptural texts that shaped ideas of homelessness and pilgrimage. The image of exile was retained in religious writings that treat the metaphoric or allegorical idea of pilgrimage (see below, pp. 109, 115–116), but I do not find it in the thoughts of real pilgrims who wrote of their travels.

The pilgrimage, an institution of the Latin Church, differed from ascetic homelessness in having a stated destination, to the Holy Land or a particular shrine; once the pilgrim arrived and worshipped, his purpose was accomplished and there was little else to do but go home. But given the great dangers of travel overseas, surely no pilgrim embarked without some doubt that he would return. The Crusades, which were a form of pilgrimage, reflect this doubt—the Crusader hoped to get back with indulgences, experiences to recount, and perhaps booty; but many died and some stayed East by choice.[53] The only voyages in which the return was an essential of the plan were practical and worldly—voyages of exploration or commerce or diplomacy, whose purpose was unfulfilled unless the traveller came back to his starting point; and these, as we shall see later, were almost never likened to a pilgrimage.

Circularity was not the form of the pilgrimage in pilgrims' minds, except *at* the destination. Some authors of pilgrimage narratives, once in Jerusalem, described the shrines in a series of "walks" or "pilgrimages," each of which ended back at a starting point. (Many of those who travelled into Egypt returned to Jerusalem before sailing, though some sailed from Alexandria or elsewhere.) There is almost always a sense of making a loop, of "going around" to the sights in Palestine, where the account of the pilgrimage ends. Such an ending strikes the modern reader as inconclusive; the works often seem to peter out—a few seem,

53. Atiya, p. 155.

and perhaps were, unfinished. But it is a misunderstanding to say the authors "lost interest" once they described the destination; that is where their interest *was*. Their eye was upon a unidirectional, linear movement, comparable to the linear movement of time in Christian historiography.[54] Yet this forward movement took pilgrims *back* in time—they viewed the sites of biblical and classical antiquity, touched and walked upon the places where Jesus or his disciples or the Virgin had been. In many accounts the pilgrims' spirits revived as they approached their destination: there was jubilation upon first seeing it from afar.[55] The literary form of the pilgrimage narratives, thus based on the form of the experience, saves the best for last in a natural climactic sequence. In Mandeville, as we will see in a moment, we get a surprise twist—a *skeptical* view of the destination and some attention to the Saracens, then a second voyage to the East. But even Mandeville, the innovator, pays no heed to the return voyage. At the end of *The Canterbury Tales* it would not therefore have surprised the medieval reader when the Host proposes that they "knit up well a greet mattere" outside their destination. And the Par-

54. See Oscar Cullman, *Christ and Time: The Primitive Christian Conception of Time and History*, trans. Floyd V. Filson, rev. ed. (Philadelphia: Westminster, 1964).

55. See Mitchell, p. 87; Prescott, p. 114. About the Canterbury pilgrimage, Ward, pp. 280–281, reports that pilgrims first saw Canterbury from a stretch of road at Harbledown; there they dismounted and made the rest of the journey on foot, those under penance removing their shoes and even putting on a hairshirt.

son specifically alludes to the one-way conception of
the Jerusalem pilgrimage when he says,

> And Jhesu for his grace wit me sende
> To shewe you the way, in this viage,
> Of thilke parfit glorious pilgrimage
> That highte Jerusalem celestial.
>
> (X. 48–51)

3.
Mandeville's Travels

I hope this capsule history of pilgrimage narratives will seem as relevant to the reader as it seems to me. The "literary" tendencies of the pilgrimage narratives did not come to the fore until the fifteenth century, but the possibilities were there all along. The pilgrim authors wrote to teach and entertain; they entertained by providing a vicarious experience. Part of that experience is religious, but the better part is "curiosity"—the interest of travellers in strange things, magnificent sights, other men's customs and beliefs. Keen observation of people and a memory of one's own experience are the skills required of such writers. In the fifteenth century the author tells about himself, his fellow travellers play a role, fights break out among them, a multiplicity of viewpoints becomes part of the story. And the experience is broadening—the traveller compares foreign lands with his own and must stop to think: the circumstance plants the seed of irony and satire. None of the pilgrim authors were poets or artists, and they weren't writing fictions. But the best of their works deserve to be called literature. That literature plays a role, though it is scarcely acknowledged, in the development of fiction.

It remained for somebody to see the literary possibilities in the genre. The first to do so was Sir John Mandeville. His *Travels,* completed (so he said) in 1356, was the classic in this tradition of writing. Originally written in Anglo-French, it was translated, often more than once, into nine languages. It was translated four times into English. Some 250 manuscripts survive, 36 in English, and it was printed again and again well into the nineteenth century.[1] Chaucer almost certainly knew it, and I believe he was influenced by it; it was written when he was an adolescent, and by the time he reached maturity he could have read it in French, Latin, or English.

But in modern times it has received—a catastrophe for such a book—a literal-minded reading. Everyone knows, now, that it is a pastiche of tales and lore taken from such authors as Boldensele, Friar Odoric, Vincent of Beauvais, Jacques de Vitry, and Haiton;[2] that the author probably never travelled East at all; that his name may be a pseudonym and the man himself not, as he claimed, an Englishman. So Mandeville has been written off as a fake; scholars condescend to him with quotes around his name and report his sources with donnish amusement. It seems (to some) merely sad or droll that he was taken seriously by Christopher Columbus, Sir Thomas More, Sir Walter Raleigh, and readers all over Europe well into the nineteenth cen-

---

1. Bennett, *The Rediscovery of Sir John Mandeville,* pp. 219–260.
2. Ibid., pp. 15–25. See also Malcolm Letts, *Sir John Mandeville: The Man and His Book* (London: Batchworth Press, 1949), pp. 29–100, and the notes in the edition by M. C. Seymour (Oxford: Clarendon Press, 1967).

tury. Recently, in a movement to revive the book, several critics have urged it upon readers as a piece of prose fiction, of "popular" literature—a <u>romance of travel,</u> in Professor Bennett's phrase.[3] But of course its contents would have seemed more probable then than now: while men still argued about antipodes and circumnavigating the globe, while they knew little about the Orient and nothing about a fourth continent or "New World," anything was possible. Their attitude might be compared to that with which men of our time read reports of space travel or flying saucers—but with an important difference: when a medieval writer transmitted without acknowledgment the words and contents of another author, he was not judged, as Mandeville has been, a fraud.

From this viewpoint Mandeville was an encyclopedist, a scholar. The virtues of his work are "humanistic" ones, those of the library and the study. He mastered an imposing amount of written matter, organized it in an original form, and presented it in a thoughtful, imaginative way that might as well be called artistic. A travel book based on learning rather than personal experience sounds like the undertaking of a humanist, and as we have seen, Petrarch himself made such an undertaking. With this in mind Zacher argues that Mandeville's "curiosity" is historically akin to the intellectual pursuits and exploratory voyages of Renaissance men: he sees in the plan of the work an embodiment of the historical movement from medieval pilgrimage to Renaissance voyage, and

3. Bennett, pp. 1–86; Seymour, pp. xvii–xx.

finds in Mandeville an inclination like Petrarch's "to make many brief visitations with maps, and books, and imagination."[4] If we look at the work this way we can see in it the kind of book that likely would have captured Chaucer's imagination, as Petrarch's and Boccaccio's books did.

The tone and style of Mandeville's book are controlled and artful. For the most part he adopts an impersonal, factual manner: "Now after that men have visited those holy places, then will they turn toward Jerusalem . . ."; "In that valley is a field where men draw out of the earth a thing that men clepe *cambyll* . . ." (9).[5] Almost everything is presented in this general, authoritative voice; it is the flat statement customary in medieval prose and much medieval poetry. The "I" in such writing is an impersonal Everyman who arranges and records truths: "I have told you now of ways by which men goeth farthest and nearest to Jerusalem. . . . Now will I tell you the right way and the shortest . . ." (14). The opening passage is devotional and exhortatory, but the rest is in the main factual and expository:

Also in that country and in other also men find long apples to sell in their season, and men clepe them apples of Paradise. And they be right sweet and of good savour, and though ye cut them in never so many gobbets or parts overthwart or endlong, evermore ye shall find in the midst the figure of the

4. Zacher, *Curiosity and Pilgrimage,* ch. 6, esp. p. 156.

5. Quotations are from the modern-spelling edition by M. C. Seymour (Oxford: Oxford University Press, 1968), based on his authoritative edition of 1967. Citations in the text are to chapters.

holy cross of Our Lord Jesus.[6] But they will rot within eight days, and for that cause men may not carry of those apples to no far countries. Of them men find the mountance of an hundred in a basket to sell. And they have great leaves of a foot and an half of length, and they be convenably large.(7)

6. An interesting detail; "apples of paradise" (bananas) are described in a number of pilgrims' accounts—Mandeville probably had the detail from Boldensele, who makes the common observation that when cut the banana shows a cross or crucifix. Mandeville appears to embroider on this by saying "overthwart or endlong" (crosswise or lengthwise), which suggests he had not really cut up a banana. But it is not quite so simple. The banana may have been different enough from the cultured fruit of today that it did seem to show a Cross in whatever direction it was cut. Whether this was so or not, people believed they saw it. Mandeville's contemporary, Niccolò of Poggibonsi, who made the journey in 1346–50, saw the Cross when the fruit was cut "lengthwise, crosswise or sidewise. . . . And this I observed well." (Elsewhere he tells us, "my companion saw a fish, which had a head like a man's, with face, mouth, teeth, nose, eyes, hair and ears, and likewise a bit of a neck; these all he had exactly like a man's and all the rest like those of a fish.") See *A Voyage Beyond the Seas (1346–1350)*, trans. T. Bellorini and E. Hoade, Publications of the Studium Biblicum Franciscanum no. 2 (Jerusalem: Franciscan Press, 1945), pp. 122, 100; his Italian version is printed in *Scelta di curiosità letterarie inedite o rare dal secolo XIII al XVII*, vols. 182–183 (Bologna, 1881). Later in the century, in 1384–85, a party of thirteen Tuscans travelled to the Holy Land, three (Leonardo Frescobaldi, Giorgio Gucci, and Simone Sigoli) returning to write accounts. Frescobaldi tells us of bananas, "They say that it is the fruit in which Adam sinned, and dividing it in any way you find a cross, and in many places we experienced this." Sigoli tells us, "Again there is a fruit on which our forefather Adam sinned . . . and they are in colour like our cucumbers. It is true they are somewhat longer and a little thinner, and they are delicate to the taste, very soft, and the taste is so different from our fruits that he who gets used to eating the said fruit, enjoys it so much as to leave everything else. In this fruit is

Mandeville was trying to write a new kind of work, a *summa* of travel lore which combined the authority of learned books and guidebooks with the eyewitness manner of pilgrim and travel writers; combined the pilgrimage to the Holy Land with the missionary or mercantile voyage into the Orient; and combined the curious and vicarious intentions of some such works with the thoughtful and devotional intentions of others. He tells us in the Prologue that he writes for the reader's "solace and comfort," adding in chapter 4 that "many men have great liking to hear speak of strange things of diverse countries"; in the last chapter he reminds us that "new things and new tidings be pleasant to hear." It is a vicarious journey, written, he says, "for as much as it is long time passed that there was no general passage nor voyage over the sea"; yet it is a guide as well, intended "specially for them, that will and are in purpose for to visit the Holy City of Jerusalem and the holy places that are thereabout" (Prologue). He addresses the reader directly as "you," inviting him into the work as a participant and promising at the end to those readers who will pray for him to "make them partners and grant them part of all the good pilgrimages and of all the good deeds that I have

---

seen a very great wonder, for when you divide it in any way, either by its length or by its breadth, whichever way you cut it, the Crucifix is distinctly to be seen inside: and in proof our company did it several times. And by many these are called Paradise apples." See *Visit to the Holy Places . . .* , trans. T. Bellorini and E. Hoade, Publications of the Studium Biblicum Franciscanum no. 6 (Jerusalem: Franciscan Press, 1948), pp. 43, 161.

done." The work is meant to delight, and its popularity shows it succeeded in this; but it is meant to teach as well—not just facts about foreign lands, but a frame of mind that Mandeville himself possessed and meant, by implication, to recommend.

The author who plans such a combination must choose some features of his models and sacrifice others, or else produce a monster. What he decides *not* to do tells much about what he did. In choosing to play the eyewitness, Mandeville sacrificed the bookish stance of citing authorities: though he had a library of travel books before him as he wrote, he concealed it, making little display of book-learning. On the other hand, he did not pretend to present day-to-day reality as if he were keeping a log. Nor did he pretend to be writing a guidebook—he sacrificed the realistic possibilities of offering tips about prices, food, contracts with mariners, and such, in favor of objective description that provides the reader with a vicarious experience. He could have put on much more of a show than he did, and his book could have been much more of a "hoax." But he was constructing a fiction, not a hoax. He chose therefore to construct a "fictive narrator," as I fear we now call it, with a particular quality: he is objective, detached, capable of providing the reader with a vicarious experience. In constructing such a fiction, he made three positive choices:

(1) He chose to maintain the stance, largely and perhaps wholly a fiction, of an eyewitness who reports from memory. This insistence that seeing is believing, this emphasis on experience at the expense of author-

ity, is what we now perceive as fictional and literary. He creates within the work a "persona" who claims firsthand knowledge of what is reported. We do not know whether this persona was like the author; that the figure is a stock knight-errant makes one dubious, for few such knights possessed his scholarship.[7] His story, discreetly parcelled out, is the stuff of romance. He is, he tells us in his Prologue, a knight ("albeit I be not worthy") who was born in England at St. Albans and went to sea on the day of St. Michael, 1322. He travelled through many lands, and proposes to report them as best he can remember. In passing, he mentions having served as a soldier to the Sultan at Babylon in his wars against the Bedouins—"And he would have married me full highly to a great prince's daughter if I would have forsaken my law and my belief, but I thank God I had no will to do it for nothing that he behight me" (6). He served the Great Chan for fifteen months against the king of Mancy. He claims that he still possesses a thorn from our Lord's crown of thorns, "that seemeth like a white thorn, and that was given to me for great speciality"(2). He claims that he saw more among the Saracens than others had seen because he had "letters of the Sultan with his great seal, and commonly other men have but his signet," which commanded men "to let me see all the places and to inform

---

7. Bennett, p. 192, thinks his learning suggests he was the younger son of a noble family. On his identity and nationality, see Bennett, pp. 181–204 and passim; on his persona in the work, p. 5. One should note that he does not represent himself in the work as being in the least bookish.

me plainly the mysteries of every place" (11). He tells of an awesome encounter he had with devils in the Valley Perilous (31).[8] At the end, reminding us of all the lands he has seen, he says he has been "at many a fair deed of arms, albeit that I did none myself for mine unable insuffisance"—an amusing touch. "Now," he concludes, "I am come home maugree myself to rest for gouts arthritic that me distrain" (34).

Only at the end do we get this picture of the aging knight with his arthritic gouts "recording the time passed." Until then, he has seemed a robust soldier-traveller, observant, open-minded, accurate, and discreet. He promises at the outset to tell "some part of things that there be, when time shall be, after it may best come to my mind." He makes no great claims for his memory and so grants—playfully, it may be—a chance of inaccuracy:

But lords and knights and other noble and worthy men that con not Latin but little and have been beyond the sea know and understand if I say truth or none. And if I err in devising for forgetting or else, that they may redress it and amend it. For things passed out of long time from a man's mind or from his sight turn soon into forgetting, because that mind of man ne may not be comprehended nor withholden for the frailty of mankind. (Prologue)

8. This is a dressed-up version of a tale in Odoric (see Bennett, pp. 46–47 and Letts, pp. 88–91). Of the events in which the author claims direct participation, this seems the most fantastic. But the reader should compare Benvenuto Cellini's encounter with devils in the Coliseum under the auspices of a gifted necromancer, in his *Autobiography*, ch. 64. Cellini appears to believe he saw devils and anticipates no skepticism on the reader's part.

His work supports this last, ambiguous statement.[9] Unable to resist a good story, he lets his tale spill over all the time into the fabulous, and at the end informs us that he has seen much more than he has told, but "it were too long thing to devise you the manner."

(2) He chose to play the objective observer, distinguishing fact from hearsay and the reasonable from the improbable. Jerusalem pilgrims did sometimes stay on to travel in the Near East, but it was a stroke of literary imagination on Mandeville's part to combine a tale of a pilgrimage (mostly Boldensele's) with one of an Oriental expedition (mostly Odoric's). This arrangement proceeds from the near to the far, from familiar things to strange ones. Everyone knew about the Holy Land because it was the locus of the Bible and the Crusades. But the Orient was a fabled place. Stories about it, even true ones, were hard to believe: so Marco Polo earned the reputation of a liar. To proceed from the Holy Land to the Orient meant leaving the world of established authority and books and pilgrims' lore for a world of stories, an insubstantial world preserved

9. *Comprehended* could mean "understood" or "contained" (as in a summary or treatise). *Withholden* could mean "kept in use" or "restrained." The phrase may hint at an overactive imagination. The Anglo-French, in Warner's edition (London: Roxburghe Club, 1889), p. 3, reads "qar choses de long temps passez par le veue tornent en obly, et memorie de homme ne peut mye tot retiner ne comprendre." Bennett, pp. 5–8, 135–146, shows that the Anglo-French (i.e., "Norman" French spoken in England after it had become dialectally differentiated from that spoken in Normandy) is the original version and that none of the English translations could have been made by the author. The ambiguity is less evident in the French but the remark could still be read as an instance of the author's sly humor.

in men's minds and memories. No one doubted it was there, or that it was inhabited, or that some had travelled to it; but the quality of this reality was different —one could find Herod in Scripture, but not Ghengis Khan. Mandeville willingly accepts this circumstance: he tells us he travelled through the Orient as far as the land of Prester John, but he makes little effort to convince us. He gives no circumstantial details of his day-to-day activities in travel, does not mention his fellow travellers or relate any personal anecdotes; the furthest he goes is to give distances between places or spans of time, to mention now and then his service as a soldier, to report his encounter with devils, and to relate conversations.

This last is the most important. He recorded judiciously what others said; we now know that he was doing this all the time, but with a stack of books. He remains calmly skeptical, plucking falsehood with diligence from the truth. He rejects out of hand the story that half the Cross is at Cyprus: "It is not so. For that cross that is in Cyprus is the cross in the which Dismas the Good Thief was hanged on" (2). He qualifies and explains: "That sea is not more red than another sea; but in some place thereof is the gravel red, and therefore men clepen it the Red Sea" (8). Even when he claims firsthand experience, as of the Well of Youth, he is cautious: "I have drunk thereof three or four sithes, and yet methinketh I fare the better" (18). He makes a great show of his reliability: "I wot never, but God knoweth" (12), "I have not been in that country . . . wherefore I may not well tell you the manner" (14), "I was not there, but it was told us" (32). About the terrestrial paradise he is especially circumspect: "Of Paradise ne can I not speak properly, for I was not there. It is far beyond, and that forethinketh me, and also I was not worthy. But as I have heard say of wise men beyond, I shall tell you with good will." "Of that place," he concludes, "I can say you no more. And therefore I shall hold me still and return to that that I have seen" (33). So, at the end: "There be many other diverse countries and many other marvels beyond that I have not seen, wherefore of them I cannot speak properly to tell you the manner of them" (34).

Such caution is rather the virtue of the scholar than of the traveller, but it was a standard attitude among the pilgrim authors, who were learned men. None wanted to be called a liar. If they included the reports of others, what doubts they cast on less credible tales made the ones they vouched for seem the more authentic. Mandeville establishes his claim to authority with such a display of candor. As we move into distant lands we encounter exotic fruits and animals, alien customs, and races of men unlike ourselves—giants with one eye, men without heads whose eyes are in their shoulders, men with horses' hoofs. They are all reported in the flat language of fact, and we are seduced into believing them because the author implies he saw them and betrays no doubts. Anything is possible, he makes us feel. In the most famous passage of the work, he urges upon us the circumnavigation of the globe—"the which thing I prove thus after that I have seen" (20). In evidence he gives astronomical observations, a computation of the earth's circumference, an empirical observation (in Jerusalem a spear stuck in the earth at noon when it is equinox makes no shadow!), a passage from the Psalms ("Deus operatus est salutem in medio terrae"), and a tale of a man who sailed until he arrived at a land where he heard his own language spoken—and then turned around and went back. It is reasonable and possible, and that is all he claims. He keeps a balance between his own credulity and the seeming fantasy of his subject matter, matching the reader's skepticism with his own. Still, Bennett has shown that Mandeville enhanced what he found in his sources with specific details artfully designed to lend authenticity.[10] And certainly he did not balk at including marvels.

(3) He chose to <u>provide a vicarious experience that calls forth a frame of mind.</u> This is by far his most important intention. He went about executing it, I believe, chiefly on instinct. He had a penchant for understatement and anticlimax. He had a habit of pairing and juxtaposing, which produced in his work a series of contrasts and contradictions. His inclination was to think and question, and he invites the reader to join him in this intellectual aspect of his journey.

Mandeville's art is one of vivid, precise detail and forthright statement, but more than that one of selection and arrangement. The most striking feature of his style is his habit of pairing things in a complementary relationship. <u>Polarities, oppositions, and "tensions"</u> are inescapable in human experience, and surely the Middle Ages had its share of them—heaven and hell, Christ and Satan, God and man, charity and cupidity,

10. Bennett, pp. 26–53.

ecclesia and *mundus*. Mandeville, though, saw things in pairs more than other medieval writers did. The first two stories in the book are an example. In chapter 4 he tells the tale of Ypocras's daughter, transformed into a dragon; every knight who looked upon her would die, but if one dared to kiss her she would be turned back to her right form and he would be lord of her kingdom. In the next chapter he tells of a damsel who died suddenly and whose lover lay with her in the tomb; from this necrophiliac union is born an adder who flies about the city, making it "sink down." Whether one interprets these two tales as folkloristic, Jungian, or "allegorical," they are neatly juxtaposed—both involve a damsel, a knight, and a fabulous creature; one is about the possible and hopeful, the other about the forbidden and dreadful; in one death may be overcome, in the other death is hideously reproduced. It would not be impossible to see in them a suggestion of salvation and damnation, spiritual life and spiritual death. At the end of the book, two tales are similarly paired. In chapter 30 is the tale of Gatholonabes's false earthly paradise, immediately following in the next chapter is that of the Valley Perilous. In the one instance a man-made heaven on earth lures some but brings others to destroy it; in the other a spot of authentic hell on earth ensnares some but leaves others, including the narrator, untempted and unharmed.

Such paired tales would be of little interest if Mandeville had not constructed the whole work on the same principle. The first fifteen chapters are an account of "the Holy Land and of that country about" (16); the remainder, an account of a voyage into "those coun-

tries beyond." The whole seems a linear, episodic narrative, combining two pre-existing genres of travel
literature, with details pilfered from many sources.
The book, for all its digressiveness, is remarkably
structured; its two parts are set against each other so as
to reveal a common truth from different perspec-
tives.[11]

Mandeville's account of the Jerusalem pilgrimage
(chapters 1–15) proceeds from the familiar to the exotic. We go from Constantinople through Greece,
Egypt, and the Holy Land, to Damascus. What people
believe is a major interest of Mandeville's, as it had
been of other pilgrim authors. The practice of Christianity becomes steadily more exotic; at the end, an
account of Saracen beliefs. His objectivity and tolerance, even to infidels, remain exemplary. Far from ex-
coriating their errors, he seems altogether optimistic
about their closeness to the truth. Perhaps he hoped for
the conversion of the Mohammedans more than for
their conquest; but he evidently believed, because he
said so, that Christians of the West should look to their
own waywardness before they aspired to take the East.
The call for a conquest of the Holy Land was a cliché of
pilgrims' accounts,[12] and Mandeville gently calls the
notion into question by suggesting that a holy war is to

11. In this I disagree, as does Zacher, with M. C. Seymour, who
in his 1967 edition, pp. xvii–xviii, argues that the author is uncon-
cerned with form. On the remainder of the book, actually the more
significant part of it, I have said more in the article from which the
present section is condensed, "The World of Mandeville's
Travels," *The Yearbook of English Studies* 1 (1971): 1–17.

12. Atiya, *The Crusade in the Later Middle Ages,* ch. 8, esp. pp.
161–165.

be fought by holy men. His plan "to show you a part of customs and manners and diversities of countries" (4) thus takes on a moral tone which reflects the reforming spirit of his age. As the lands and customs become more exotic, the contrast with Catholic Europe becomes greater; whatever good we find in outlandish men, whatever truth we find in their false doctrines, must give us pause. At the end of the pilgrimage the Sultan's long catalogue of Christians' sins thus stands out as a rebuke to Western Christendom. So too, at the very end of the work, when he arrives at the far reaches of the Orient, Mandeville finds men who follow a natural, primitive form of Christianity.

Mandeville takes great pains to lead up to his conclusion about Mohammedans. The pilgrimage, like all such accounts, is an itinerary, its organization dictated by geography and chronology. But he imposes on his linear narrative several motifs that give it a sense of progression. For example, as he examines the shrines of the Holy Land, episodes of the Gospels naturally come into play, and he arranges these so that they endue the high point of the pilgrimage with an undertone of redemptive history. In chapter 9, at Bethlehem, the birth of Christ hovers in the background; in chapter 11, the Crucifixion; in chapter 12, at the river Jordan, John the Baptist and the Baptism of Jesus, which suggests conversion and salvation; in chapter 13, at Galilee where Antichrist will be born, the Day of Judgment.

A similar effect is attained by the alphabets Mandeville dispersed through the account of the pilgrimage: they become, like the lands which use them, progressively more exotic. In chapter 3 the Greek alphabet, in 7 the "Egyptian" (Coptic, very garbled), in 12 the Hebrew, in 15 the Arabic. Each comes at the end of a chapter, and so the last comes at the tail end of the pilgrimage: Mandeville, commenting that the Arabic has four letters which other alphabets do not have, adds that "we in England" have two that they do not have, thorn and yogh. The detail, placed strategically last, suggests that "our" alphabet would seem as strange to them as theirs to us.

The venture into the Holy Land thus becomes a mirror in which the "true" Christian of the West sees himself reflected: different in beliefs and customs, with the advantage of the true faith and true church, but not better in practicing this faith. Bloomfield finds in this feature of Mandeville's book a sense of history and cultural diversity.[13] From scholastic philosophy medieval men had learned of a "natural religion" implanted in all men's reason. Some came to believe it was possible for all men to know the truth in some murky way, and the idea made them more tolerant and more curious toward infidels and schismatics. This sense of cultural diversity spurred the spirit of reform. Few medieval men, however curious about strange lands, doubted that the Church of Rome was the true church and its dogmas the true faith; there is not a scrap of evidence that Mandeville entertained such doubts, though an earlier editor, Hamelius, advanced elaborate

13. Morton W. Bloomfield, "Chaucer's Sense of History," *Journal of English and Germanic Philology* 51 (1952): 301–313, rpt. in *Essays and Explorations* (Cambridge, Mass.: Harvard University Press, 1970), pp. 12–26; see pp. 23–24.

arguments to that effect. But men's failure to live up to the advantages of the true church distressed earnest Christians of the West, and some contemplated in their imaginations the simple and good intentions of the misguided in the East.

One way Mandeville makes this point is in his treatment of relics. Relics have been called the true religion of the late Middle Ages, which was perhaps so at the popular level; but they were still a scandal. Erasmus's famous spoof in his *Colloquies* had a long tradition behind it, the Pardoner's "pigges bones" being one example. In spite of abuses, however, the Canterbury pilgrimage existed because the saint's body lay in the Cathedral, the Jerusalem pilgrimage because that was the soil the Lord had walked upon. Mandeville is very respectful of true relics, and eager to inform the reader which are authentic. Of the Templum Domini in Jerusalem he says, "In this temple was Charlemagne when that the angel brought him the prepuce of Our Lord Jesus Christ of His circumcision. And after King Charles let bring it to Paris into his chapel, and after that he let bring it to Poitiers and after that to Chartres" (11). In chapter 12 he gives a detailed account of the head of St. John the Baptist: its hinder part is at Constantinople, the forepart to the chin at Rome, the jaws at Genoa. But then he comes to the point: "And some men say that the head of St. John is at Amiens in Picardy, and other men say that it is the head of St. John the bishop. I wot never, but God knoweth. But in what wise that men worship it the blessed St. John holdeth him apaid." By heaping up a charnelhouse of specific details, Mandeville shows that the relics are dispersed all over Europe and in their wake a thousand rival claims; behind them, he suggests, is a spiritual and historical reality—saints who walked the earth as men, whose lives are preserved in the story of the Christian faith, and who, from heaven, see into our hearts.

The Holy Land is presented as a relic of sorts. The long list of places and shrines there is disjunctive and unstructured. Each site takes its meaning from its part in the Old or New Testament, in the Christian story. The reader's familiarity with this story is taken for granted. The way places now look is not glossed over, and the distance between the present and the biblical past is emphasized:

After go men by the hill beside the plains of Galilee unto Nazareth, where was wont to be a great city and a fair but now there is not but a little village and houses abroad here and there. And it is not walled, and it sitteth in a little valley and there be hills all about. There was Our Lady born. . . . (13)

The style of these passages (9–14), with its paratactic sentence structure, its *and*'s and jumble of details, is especially appropriate. We see, as one would on pilgrimage, towns and shrines all helter-skelter, learn odd bits of information and glimpse curiosities as we pass. The disjunctive reality of things seen and reported is like scales before our eyes, which we must remove to see their meaning. All tangible, visible things pertinent to the faith take their meaning from the Bible and from the faith of individual Christians. At the end of the pilgrimage, we learn to our discomfort, the Saracens say that Christian men "be cursed also . . . for they keep not the commandments and the precepts of the gospel that Jesus Christ taught them" (15).

The second half of the book, from chapter 16 on, is a voyage into the Orient, but it is integrated with the first part in a remarkable way and differs from other members of its genre precisely because it is cast in the form of a quasi- or anti-pilgrimage through a state of nature. We pass beyond the land of Prester John to a shrine one may not enter: "Paradise Terrestre, where that Adam our foremost father and Eve were put that dwelled there but little while, and that is towards the east at the beginning of the earth" (33). The pilgrimage to Jerusalem was a journey backward in time: one saw relics of New and Old Testament times, what the Middle Ages would have called the Age of Grace and the Age of Law (that is, the law of Moses). Mandeville keeps this reverse order: in the second part we learn that Noah's ship is on Mt. Ararat; that each of Noah's sons inhabited one of the three continents, Asia, Africa, and Europe; that the round earth was wasted by Noah's flood; that there is a lake in Ceylon where Adam and Eve wept a hundred years. In this world of the distant past lies the dispersal of individuals, peoples, and languages; at the root of all, the expulsion from Paradise. We pass through the leavings of the *first* age of the world, the age before the law of Moses, the Age of Nature.

It is, however, *fallen* nature, nature in decline from its primeval state—a world of grotesques, sports and freaks of nature, of anthropophagi and men whose heads do grow beneath their shoulders—along with strange animals (giant snails, geese with two heads, griffins), trees that bear venom, wine, wool. It is the world of Bosch and Breughel; but in this world Mandeville shows us kingdoms of high civilization that practice a "natural" religion and "natural" virtues. He finds peoples who go naked, practice communal sexuality, communism of lands and goods, idolatry, cremation, polygamy, cannibalism—and practice these because of their beliefs and doctrines, which he treats with characteristic tolerance. Below them are peoples too close to animals to *have* beliefs—dog-headed men, men with horses' hoofs or trunks, men who hiss like snakes or grunt like pigs. In chapters 25–26 we learn of the history, governance, law, and customs of the Great Chan, the "greatest lord under the firmament," who tolerates Christianity and permits conversions among his subjects; as do the Tartars.

That there is religious freedom in this world of nature makes it very different from the world of grace in Western Europe, land of Crusades and Inquisitions, and the point was not lost on Mandeville. In two passages he describes religions that parody Christianity—parody the death-loving, pessimistic side of medieval Christianity with its emphasis on martyrdom, "mortification," "contempt of the world." We encounter "saints" who kill themselves for the love of an idol; their kinsmen who collect and worship the "saint's" relics; women who weep when their children are born because they have come into a world of sorrow, and who throw themselves and their children on their husbands' funeral pyres. In such passages Mandeville is leading up to his grand finale, the Isle of

Brahmins, which will by contrast seem utopian. Whereas in the Holy Land, at the heart of Christendom, we found Saracens, at the earth's end, in the state of nature, we find a simplified, primeval Christianity. There is the land of Prester John, who is Christian, whose people sing mass as the Apostles did, "as our Lord taught them" (32), without later additions, and have "a good faith natural." After this Mandeville comes to a great darkness: beyond it is the Earthly Paradise from which flow the four rivers—high, walled, covered with moss, having a single entrance barred by fire, which none can enter.

Then in the last chapter, in the kind of anticlimax for which Mandeville had a taste, we get a startling turn-about: on the Isle of Rybothe (Tibet) is a religion pointedly like the Roman Church, having a pope and a fantastic cannibal rite that seems a nightmare version of the Christian mass. When a man dies, his son has the body decapitated and fed in pieces to birds (which in their liturgy are called angels to God). The son at a feast then serves the flesh of his father's head to special friends and makes of the skull a cup, and they drink "with great devotion in remembrance of the holy man that the angels to God have eaten. And that cup the son shall keep to drink of all his lifetime in remembrance of his father." This passage, which sounds from one point of view like an acerb parody of Christian beliefs and practices, reintroduces the theme of cannibalism; but here it is shorn of any destructive or aggressive motive, impregnated with filial piety, with tenderness, with dignified family love, and redolent of the Holy Communion even down to the echo of Christ's injunction, "Do this in remembrance of Me."[14] It is one of the most startling passages in English literature, a turning-about of accustomed values which mocks nothing, but questions everything. It asks us to behold a cannibalism not savage or repugnant but tender, dignified, and pious. It subtly reminds us of the Christian rites at which the Body and Blood of the Lord are consumed, but throws attention upon the spirit in which men perform such rites. Mandeville expresses no repugnance whatever at this curious antisacrament (Odoric called it, and made it seem, "vile and abominable"). Like other passages it makes the customs of the East a distorted reflection of the West, forcing a comparison of the two.

Mandeville's art in leading the reader behind a cultural institution to moral and spiritual essentials makes him seem a social critic or a satirist. It is possible—some have done it—to take such a view too far, to make him a More or Swift with specific axes to grind. Yet his work is more like other such accounts of his time than like a later utopia or satire. If his book is ironic it is because travel itself is ironic: things are other than what we expect at home, and the contrast turns us back upon ourselves. Mandeville grasped this instructive feature of travelling better than previous authors. Perhaps because he saw from afar, through a world of books, he saw more thoughtfully. Zacher styles him a *curiosus,* an intellectual, an observer and reader whose keenness led him to contemplate distant lands and the

14. Mandeville developed a hint in Friar Odoric, ch. 15, who refers to "their pope." Bennett, p. 47 n. 25, identifies the supposedly Tibetan funeral service as a Zoroastrian custom.

circumnavigation of the globe, and the wonder and promise of creation.[15] But at the key moments of his narrative he turns his eyes within, for he is no less curious about the essentials of man's life than about the corners of the globe.

Mandeville's ideas were respectable ideas of his time, and his spirit was large enough to encompass them in their full complexity. He would have Western Christians conquer the Holy Land and convert the East, but not without examining and reforming their own lives—and they could learn to do so even from heathens. On one side, his idea of reform tends to a brand of primitivism which supposes a pristine faith and simple virtues among "natural" men. On the other side, though in the latter part of his book he sees the corrupted world in decline from its first age, he rejects extremes of self-abnegation and self-destruction, placing value upon civilization, government, learning. He is an enthusiast of travel who would have men of the future sail about the earth; but the fragmented curiosities, the relics and ruins that the voyager observes, have their *meaning* from the past, and the past is known to us from books.

15. Zacher, esp. pp. 141–157.

4.
Chaucer

The Canterbury Tales is almost never considered a fictional piece of travel literature. Since Dryden's time it was thought modelled on the *Decameron,* and when that opinion was discarded in the middle of the nineteenth century it was still thought similar in kind: a "frame-story" or frame narrative. This has had the status of fact since Robert Pratt and Karl Young compared it with other frame narratives and, finding it dissimilar, attested to Chaucer's originality.[1] In such a comparison, the *Decameron* and Sercambi's *Novelle* seem to get the highest marks for points in common, with *The Divine Comedy,* the *Roman de la Rose,* and Gower's *Confessio Amantis* following in that order. Those at least are the results I get. Compared with such books, only one feature of the work has no precedent: that the setting is a pilgrimage.[2] Everyone agrees it was

1. "The Literary Framework of the Canterbury Tales," in W. F. Bryan and Germaine Dempster, eds., *Sources and Analogues of Chaucer's Canterbury Tales* (1941; rpt. New York: Humanities Press, 1958), pp. 1–33.
2. It is often wrongly assumed that the journey in Sercambi's *Novelle* is a pilgrimage. An earlier version, the *Novelliero* (ca. 1374), is lost; there are two accounts of it but neither says anything about a pilgrimage—one calls it "un viaggio per la Toscana" (see Bryan and Dempster, eds., *Sources and Analogues,* p. 29). The *Novelle,*

a remarkable stroke on Chaucer's part that he gave this special form to his collection of tales. But almost no one ever seriously thinks of *The Canterbury Tales* as a story about a pilgrimage: it would be naive. Hence no one has viewed accounts of pilgrimages as analogues.[3] Of course the *metaphor* of the pilgrimage occurs in works Chaucer knew, like the *Pélérinage de la vie humaine, The Divine Comedy,* and the *Roman*. But what Chaucer describes is an actual group of people on an actual journey.

When Chaucer hit upon the Canterbury pilgrimage as the form of a frame narrative, then, he did something inventive. He presented it not as local color but in its full cultural context—in its historical, ideological, and spiritual dimensions. And he made it central. It

---

which Chaucer might have seen, is never called a pilgrimage, has no destination or religious purpose; the purpose is to escape the plague, as in the *Decameron*. The company goes down the west coast of Italy and up the east coast, tours the north, and ends outside Lucca where it began—rather, the manuscript breaks off there. Clearly the company was meant to return home (see *Sources and Analogues,* pp. 24–25); this, as we have seen, was not the model of the pilgrimage.

3. Edmund Reiss, in "The Pilgrimage Narrative and the *Canterbury Tales,* " *Studies in Philology* 67 (1970): 295–305, like his predecessors Baldwin and Robertson, is chiefly interested in the allegorical or metaphoric character of the pilgrimage, on which see also Charles P. R. Tisdale, "The Medieval Pilgrimage and Its Use in *The Canterbury Tales*" (Ph.D. diss., Princeton, 1970), esp. chs. 2 and 3, and F. C. Gardiner, *The Pilgrimage of Desire: A Study of Theme and Genre in Medieval Literature* (Leiden: E. J. Brill, 1971), esp. ch. 1. But one would never know from these treatments of the pilgrimage metaphor that medieval pilgrims packed up and went to real places.

is the first detail he gives—the first main clause of the work singles it out:

> Than longen folk to goon on pilgrimages
> And palmers for to seeken straunge strondes
> To ferne halwes, kouth in sundry londes . . .[4]

The passage, with its mention of palmers, foreign shores, and distant shrines, refers specifically to the Jerusalem pilgrimage, the prototype of pilgrimages, before it mentions Canterbury. When the pilgrims are in sight of their destination, the Parson reminds them again of the glorious pilgrimage of human life "that highte Jerusalem Celestial."

Having "framed" his work with these references to the prototype of pilgrimages, however, Chaucer in some sense violates our expectations by giving us the local, national pilgrimage to Canterbury—a choice not unlike Boccaccio's and Sercambi's excursions out of the plague-ridden city. Then he violates our expectations further by withholding local color and circumstantial detail: we are not aware of horses, blessings, souvenirs or badges or trappings appropriate to pilgrims; there are no overnight stops, no cities are passed through, the destination is never reached. About all this I have shot off my whole load of ammunition elsewhere, and it need not concern us here.[5] The pilgrimage is eerily symbolic when you squint and see the whole; but from moment to moment, what

---

4. Quotations are in normalized spelling according to the principles stated by me and James Dean in our Signet editions of *The Canterbury Tales* (1969) and *Troilus and Criseyde* (1976).

5. *The Idea of the Canterbury Tales,* esp. pp. 159–173.

is reported—the persons and their talk—seems very factual indeed.

Whether Chaucer had read any factual accounts of pilgrimages or travels we cannot be sure, but it stands to reason that he had. There were many of them, he was himself a seasoned traveller, and he was an avid reader with an interest in geography and cosmography. The one literary or "humanistic" account, the first that could be reckoned a work of fiction, *Mandeville's Travels,* was widely read, and Professor Bennett notes an echo from it in the Squire's Tale.[6] But even if Chaucer had never read any such works, they show what kind of account medieval pilgrims wrote, what form the age imposed on such material. They are useful as analogues of the whole book because what Chaucer wrote has many points in common with them. In what follows I am going to examine some of these points with an eye to differences. In each respect, Chaucer enlarges upon the tendencies of the pilgrimage narratives, vivifies, enhances. He makes his pilgrimage everywhere more extravagant, more thoughtful, more dramatic than the true stories of pilgrimages, just as he had done in the *Troilus* with the "matere" of *Il Filostrato*. He converts the factual account to a poetical and fictional one, an artifice whose truth is owing not to "real life" but to the life of the mind.

Chaucer made his work literary in a fully conscious way. It is almost entirely in verse. It begins in the high style, parading springtime conventions and learned

6. Bennett, *The Rediscovery of Sir John Mandeville,* pp. 224–227.

A.P. Newton. ed. Travel & Travellers in MA (London. 1926)

Jerusalem (WB
       −3 times

Pilgrimage
 — Metaphor
 — Spiritual exercise

                            1100 − 1500 − 526 accounts

Canterbury — 200,000 per annum
Compostella
Rome

Pelerinage de la vie humaine
Divine Comedy
Roman de la Rose

references. It introduces a narrator not identical with the author, and describes a company that represents the society of the day. Its "matere" is stories—some "literary" like the Knight's, some mock-literary like *Sir Thopas,* some drawn from legend, folk tale, and fabliau; all are made literary by his transforming hand. Some are pieced together into dramatic and thematic groups. The whole, unlike any pilgrimage narrative, is planned on literary models: it has a beginning, middle, and end, and is intended for "sentence and solaas"—to teach and delight.

The pilgrim authors did nothing like this. Whether we can call their works literature is a matter of definition—certainly they would not *then* have been reckoned literary. They are never written in verse. Those in the vernacular have a workaday prose style intended for practical informative purposes; those in Latin are almost never high-flown. Since they are by churchmen intended mostly for other churchmen, they adopt off and on the garden-variety rhetoric of ecclesiastical or monastic circles; Paul Walther's preface, for example, echoes with bombastic *heu*'s and *o*'s, but the rest is plainspoken. The authors do not see their audience as a literary one, do not anticipate on the reader's part much interest in style or rhetorical "colors." They anticipate interest and curiosity. Johannes Phocas, writing at the end of the twelfth century, said he wrote for those who had never been on the pilgrimage, or for those who had, "if it be pleasant to listen to accounts of what it is enjoyable to behold." In the thirteenth century Marco Polo collaborated with a romance writer and forfeited his credibility. Ludolph, in the middle of the fourteenth century, supposed "ignorant cavillers and scoffers" among his readership. Bertrandon, writing in the fifteenth century, declared he was addressing future Crusaders and travellers, but he wanted to interest them in the voyage as much as to inform them about it; he begged to be excused if he did not write as well as others. None, except perhaps mad Margery Kempe, let posterity loom very large in their thoughts. Most were ingenuous; they wanted to share their journeys with others, wanted to appeal to the reader's curiosity, to inform him, to provide him with a vicarious experience. Almost all wanted very much to be believed.

Mandeville and Chaucer alone transformed this tradition of earnest reportage into fiction, but Mandeville's intentions are a puzzle. He seems to have wanted a wide audience: he tells us he wrote in French rather than Latin because more people knew French. [7] He was not given to rhetorical flourishes but *was* given to effects of verisimilitude and to marvels. In some part of his mind he may have viewed it as a joke—what we would call a "put-on"—expecting it to deceive gullible readers and amuse sophisticated ones, to tease the reader's credulity. If so, it is in part a parody of pilgrimage and voyage writings. Its "cultural relativism" is quasi-satiric in its effect: it asks the Christian reader to look as if from outside at the practice of Christianity

7. Bennett, p. 6, shows that the passage was garbled in the English translation. The translator had it that Mandeville first wrote in Latin and then translated into French; he added that Mandeville translated the work again out of French into English. What Mandeville wrote was "I should have written it in Latin."

in Western Europe and so to look at himself. That it *has* this effect does not of course prove the author intended it consciously. The "I" of the book behind whom lurks an author not yet identified and perhaps pseudonymous is, willy-nilly, a literary creation, a fictional narrator. The work, for all its diversity, holds together like a work of art. And its world is, we now know, a world of tales.

There is something about *The Canterbury Tales,* though, that has no counterpart in travel literature, not even in Mandeville. It has self-awareness, shows a tendency to raise questions about the nature and uses of literature itself. In it are placed two prose pieces, both moral in character and didactic in intent. These nonliterary, instructional pieces make a contrast to the rest; they introduce the dichotomy of poetry versus prose, fiction versus exposition, and so display the difference between "poetic truth" and truth expressly stated. The most outrageous tale, and one of the most successful from a literary view, is the Pardoner's sermon, a stark contrast to the Parson's "sermon" in prose (partly a scolding that might be compared with the Sultan's "sermon" at the end of Mandeville's pilgrimage). The *Melibee,* also in prose, is in essence a fable, like many of the tales, but explicitly allegorized and abounding in wise counsel, whereas the poetical tales are allegorical by subtle implication if at all, and provide wise counsel by indirection more than by statement.

The author-narrator frets over the frivolous and bawdy content of his work and excuses himself by claiming to repeat the pilgrims' words as spoken, so as not to "feine thing, or finde wordes newe." Yet as he

proceeds to imagine the pilgrims and *find* new words
for their tales, he presents most of them as artists-in-
little. They are no less anxious than he over their art.
Thus the Knight excuses himself as he goes along for
failing to write or rhyme adequately or for omitting
certain matters. The Miller will "quit" the Knight's
tale, which he parodies. The Reeve insists that what he
tells is "veray sooth." The Man of Law begins with a
pompous literary disquisition, ceding rhyme to Chaucer and claiming to speak in prose. The pilgrims are
terribly conscious of their ability to tell a story or select one. The Pardoner, a professional, brags about
technique and gives a demonstration. The Wife, by
contrast, free-associates with wondrous garrulity and
falls victim to the world of books, unable to put St.
Jerome and Theophrastus and Ovid out of mind. The
Clerk, dutiful graduate student that he is, identifies his
source. The Merchant must stop and beg to be excused
for plain speaking—he is a "rude man." The Squire,
like his father, apologizes for his inadequacies, and the
Franklin for his "rude speeche"—"I lerned never
rhetoric, certain." The narrator himself tells a tale so
bad it must be stopped (behind it, the author, parody-
ing bourgeois metrical romances, then substitutes a
"litel thing in prose" to be taken in earnest). And so it
goes—the Monk defines tragedy, the Nun's Priest
pokes fun at rhetoric. It is not surprising to find one
critic arguing that the series of tales from the Shipman's through the Nun's Priest's constitutes a "literature group" in which the Host acts as editor and critic,
the tales exploring the nature of storytelling and the

relation of "mirth" and "doctrine."[8] Implicit in much of *The Canterbury Tales,* as in many literary works, is a level of consciousness in which the author ruminates on literature and language—on his own purpose and vocation. This doesn't mean *The Canterbury Tales* is about itself or about literature. But its author did select the one activity of pilgrims most interesting to him, telling stories. It is scarcely surprising that we catch him out sometimes ruminating on "poetic truth."

In this literary conception, Chaucer capitalized on the possibilities of the narrative "I" as no writer had done before. The pilgrim authors used "I" and "we" regularly, though there were third-person accounts and impersonal guidebooks. In the twelfth century this "I" is little personalized; in the thirteenth and four-teenth centuries there are more personal touches—eyewitness accounts, anecdotes, apostrophes, excla-mations, moments of meditating or ruminating, bits of quotidian and domestic realism. The "I" comes (as it did in the romance) to be a person; we experience the journey through his eyes, and the exotic sights—the camels and pyramids and slave auctions—are the more real because he saw them himself. We hear his voice; his account is a monologue, sometimes a soliloquy. Some authors acknowledge that their audiences are stay-at-homes, and this puts distance between us and the exotic subject matter; we never quite forget we were not there. The authors never address us directly,

8. Alan T. Gaylord, *"Sentence* and *Solaas* in Fragment VII of the *Canterbury Tales:* Harry Bailly as Horseback Editor," *PMLA* 82 (1967): 226–235.

never invite us into the work with a "you," almost
never except by accident reveal any individualizing
traits about themselves. We share with them the bond
of literate people who read books and know Latin; we
are, it is taken for granted, Christians. But we do not
get to know them or share their world except at a
distance. They never play a role for us, except such a
role as they played day by day: put cheery Brother
Felix beside somber Brother Ricoldus and you see two
different worlds, the one full of excitement and danger
and sentiment, the other intellectual, objective, stern.
But neither gives us this picture of himself for artistic
effect. Mandeville is the exception. He saw the advantage of putting on a mask, though a crude one
fashioned after the knight-errant of romance and the
nearly faceless travellers whose accounts he knew. He
addressed the reader as "you." And like Chaucer he
used the pretense of remembered personal experience
to conceal the pile of books at his elbow.

The Chaucerian narrator has been an *idée fixe* of
Chaucer criticism for twenty years; we know, now, all
about its development in the early love poems, its subtle variations from one work to the other, its "func-
tions." But the obtuse dreamer of *The Book of the
Duchess,* the hapless space traveller of *The House of
Fame,* the bookish pedant of the *Troilus,* the wide-eyed
pilgrim of *The Canterbury Tales*—all these "roles" are
humorous exaggerations of the author's own experience, isolated and blown up for each occasion: he made
a game of his own obtuseness, haplessness, bookishness, naiveté. The common denominator is the man
himself, what we surmise about him—his modesty,

his self-humor, his tact. That he is a serious man who thinks deeply and sees the bleakness of the world, we know from reading his works. What he *shows* us of himself is the well-meaning but bumbling side, which most of us try to conceal. The Host (VII. 695–706) notes he is forever staring at the ground, is fat; he tells a bad tale—he is sorry, he will try to do better. In the General Prologue he lets us participate in the pleasant relationship of listener and storyteller, and flatters our vanity by making us think ourselves smarter. Then he puts himself in our role as a listener and lets others tell the tales. No pilgrimage narrator ever turned the tables on himself this way or played such games with the reader: they were serious men and were telling true stories. Chaucer brings his own credulity to center stage and treats it, as one suspects Mandeville did, playfully. In convincing us he reports the truth, he tips his hand and shows himself a liar.

By thus exploiting the possibilities of the narrative "I," Chaucer assigned the reader an active role, that of a fellow listener and judge. The narrator's objectivity and ingenuousness, the familiarity of the setting, the place names, the circumstantial details—all are meant to convince us that the pilgrimage and pilgrims are real. Professor Manly and more recently Professor Williams were so far convinced as to seek out the originals.[9] In part they were right—at least there *was* a real Harry Bailly who owned a real Tabard, and perhaps contemporaries could have made an informed guess

9. John Matthews Manly, *Some New Light on Chaucer* (New York: Henry Holt, 1926); George Williams, *A New View of Chaucer* (Durham, N.C.: Duke University Press, 1965).

about the Man of Law (who names Chaucer and alludes to Gower). But in this aura of verisimilitude, Chaucer parades unabashed fictions. The "I" of the opening lines, the familiar voice of the poet, quickly turns into a masquerade, and the masquerade-figure, the "narrator," is so uncritical that we distrust him. This unreliable narrator then begins to report details which a returned traveller could not know except on hearsay and surmise—he knows what the Monk thought, how the Pardoner felt as he rose to preach, the way the Prioress behaved in her convent. He is able to feel their feelings and think their thoughts, and so establishes for us, inside the work, the "intersubjectivity" that we experience as readers.

But his omniscience rouses the skepticism that it is natural to feel about intersubjectivity: we can never be sure we do successfully share the consciousness of others, and can never do so anyway except in part. In addition, he does not propose to retell or recreate the pilgrims' tales but makes the most outrageous truth-claim imaginable, that he can *remember* them all verbatim:

> But first I pray you of your curteisye
> That ye n'arette it not my vilainye
> Though that I plainly speke in this mattere
> To telle you hir wordes and hir cheere,
> Ne though I speke hir wordes proprely.
> For this ye knowen also well as I:
> Whoso shall tell a tale after a man,
> He moot reherce as neigh as ever he can
> Everich a word, if it be in his charge—
> Al speke he never so rudelich and large—

Or elles he moot tell his tale untrewe,
Or feine thing, or finde wordes newe.

(I. 725–736)

The claim that he does not feign anything or "finde wordes newe" is repeated by some of the pilgrims who claim, as the Reeve does, that "this is veray sooth that I you telle." But a "Canterbury tale" *meant* a tall tale;[10] the tales-within-a-tale are from an acknowledged world of fiction, a fact self-evident in a tale like the Nun's Priest's, granted by some pilgrims (for example the Clerk, who tells us he has his tale from Petrarch), and obvious anyway since all but two are in verse. Even the circumstances under which the tales were told are blatantly fictional: either they were told aloud on horseback to a group of thirty riding through open country, or they would have required some fifteen stops a day.

The pilgrim authors played no such game with false truth-claims. Each work, if not a guidebook, was a memoir. The authors had made the journey and seen the shrines themselves: like the Wife of Bath—herself a pilgrim who has been three times to Jerusalem—they put experience over authority. Some authors, like Brocardus, boasted that they told nothing they had not

10. Watt, *Canterbury Pilgrims and Their Ways,* p. 50. See *The House of Fame,* line 2122, and the note in the second edition of F. N. Robinson (Boston: Houghton Mifflin, 1957). The usage is reported in the *OED* only in the sixteenth century; but the notion that pilgrims' and travellers' tales were tall tales was firmly established. Erasmus, in the colloquy "De visendo loca sacra," suggests that all pilgrims are liars, and describes the pleasure of returning and meeting in groups to take turns and compete in telling whoppers.

seen with their own eyes. Those who admit details from "ancient history" and "truthful men" bring us to the threshold of disbelief. Mandeville steps beyond that threshold, claiming to have seen fantastic wonders of the kind that invite skepticism—he does not, perhaps, entirely expect us to believe him, but he makes his own show of skepticism when reporting what he only heard. The pilgrim authors were apprehensive about being doubted: like Ludolph, they could tell more but for ignorant scoffers and cavillers. There is a neat ambivalence in such narratives because the most interesting details, the "curious" ones, are the least believable. One way out, which the authors often take, is the scholar's way: report accurately what others say and let *them* bear the burden of proof. The other way out, which Mandeville and Chaucer take, is the ironic way: tell fictions, but tease the audience with circumstantial details and an earnest manner.

The effect of this ironic game is to make us ask where the truth lies. The pilgrim authors took the truth for granted: the Holy Land itself shimmered with meaning for every Christian. They needed only to convince their readers that they had been there themselves; hence they included details, curiosities, anecdotes. Mandeville involved and challenged the reader by questioning the standard pieties, making us see the virtues of strange lands, making us wonder whether their conquest or conversion is quite so pressing, whether first we should not reform ourselves, whether the truth is as simple as it seems. Chaucer accomplishes something like this but he reverses the method. He puts the place close to home where it can be taken for granted, makes the pilgrimage obviously unreal, sets us loose in the world of story. The narrator acts as a counterpart of the reader, a member of an audience within the poem; the Host acts as a counterpart judge. Both are mirror images which reverse our sense of ourselves: the narrator remembers everything, the Host judges naively—how unlike us. (Chaucer had fashioned this device in the *Troilus,* where the narrator is like us a reader, and Pandarus a manipulator and observer, like us a vicarious participant.) The narrator of *The Canterbury Tales* believes, responds, empathizes, and remembers, as we are expected to do. The suspension of disbelief, the imaginative response, empathy—all the requirements imposed on a reader of fiction—are thus established inside the work: the narrator does it all for us in caricature, and we need only accept him, if we can, to accept the rest. But he leaves to us what he and the Host too pointedly lack—the art of discrimination. The difference between true and false, right and wrong, good art and bad is put in our hands.

By thus involving the reader, Chaucer made his pilgrimage not merely a vicarious experience but a game. The pilgrim authors, once they got the hang of it, gave their readers a vicarious experience by letting them know what the journey was really like, by depicting its dark underside—the ubiquitous thievery, the stench of the galleys, the awful food, the bad condition of shrines. A few authors were so wrapped up in their own experience that they told little at all about what they saw. The hysterical Margery Kempe made everything the occasion or setting of her persecution; we only see her visions, hear her incessant weeping and screaming. Paul Walther lived so much in his own world that his work shades off into autobiography. Other works manage a vicarious experience without the personal tone and "quotidian domestic realism." The *Information for Pilgrims* makes an effort to do so by providing a third-person account of the visits "certain pilgrims" made to the standard shrines, though it succeeds better in this, perhaps, where it gives practical advice about money, sickness, vermin. Descriptive detail reported as accurately as the writer knows how is the essence of verisimilitude in voyage literature. And verisimilitude is the easiest way to give the reader a vicarious experience. Still, detail recorded well is never wholly "objective"; it cries out for impressions, metaphors, and emotional responses, and so invites an authorial voice.

Mandeville discovered in this circumstance its playful possibilities, but Chaucer took advantage of those possibilities as no one ever had before. Into the vicarious experience he admitted the traveller's experience of his companions, and theirs of him. The pilgrim authors showed little interest in their fellow pilgrims, and rarely had a pilgrim speak his mind or tell a story. Only in the fifteenth century do we begin to get a picture of the other pilgrims, or detailed accounts of the frequent quarrels among them. The same was true of narratives within a narrative; there is only the tendency, in those authors who report things they heard from others. Mandeville took advantage of this by letting his pilgrimage blossom into a phantasmagoria of hearsay. Some of this he claims as firsthand knowledge; he lays the rest at the door of those he listened to. Chaucer went much further. He makes dialogue and monologue central: he spotlights the pilgrims and their tales and lets the pilgrimage itself fall into the shadows. The order of tales, in many instances, follows from the spontaneous dialogue among the pilgrims, their clashes of personality, their natural enmities and grudges, their disagreements—from the shaping force of group dynamics. And Chaucer supplies a credulous fellow traveller who is just what every tale-teller yearns for: a good, a *total* listener.

Chaucer's pilgrimage is of course a game of storytelling arranged by the Host; this game is a legacy from Boccaccio, Sercambi, and other writers of frame narratives. But Chaucer makes this literal game an experience that goes beyond the element of game or play found in all fiction. He makes the game plan inside the work a counterpart of the more elaborate game that we are called upon to play as we read it. The game inside the work fails to follow its stated rules, has to be adapted to turnabouts and surprises—it becomes a game of chance. And this is true of the game we play with the author—it becomes a shill game, a guessing game or masquerade in which we are not always sure who it is we are playing with, what rules we are following, what is make-believe and what is not.

Chaucer approached this conception as an ironist and satirist. His bent, as we see in his earlier works, was toward parody and ironic commentary. The pilgrim authors shared this bent only in a left-handed way. They could not resist commenting on what they saw and experienced, and like all travellers they were great fault-finders. The venality of sailors or innkeepers or donkey-men, the errors of the infidels—all this comes in for plenty of criticism. Even in the most straightforward guidebook good advice implies bad experience: the reader, warned to make a firm contract with the ship captain requiring him not to delay sailing or stop at unnecessary ports, has learned something unflattering to ship captains. The author's fellow travellers get their share of disapproval: thievery aboard ship, Friar Felix reported, affected almost everyone, and the more circumstantial accounts produced a *dramatis personae* of nuisances—the loud-mouth, the pompous noble, the arrogant bishop, thieving sailors and galley slaves, heavy snorers. In the fifteenth century we get detailed pictures of young noblemen vying with each other over the elegance and costliness of their candles. Priests fall at each others' throats and fight for their turns to say mass at the altar of the Holy Sepulchre. Others, pretending to be deep in their devotions, covertly carve their names or coats of arms on the shrines.[11]

Then, too, travel itself naturally invites comparison and evaluation; perhaps that is why it is thought broadening. All that is strange in customs and manners and beliefs cries out for comment. At the shrine itself, on pilgrimage, one worshipped, but along the way "curiosity" made one react and so temperaments came into play; where one traveller finds exotic customs and ideas sympathetic, another and no less perennial type finds everything better back home. Still another finds

11. Felix Fabri, LPPTS, 8, pp. 346, 383; 9, pp. 86–88.

the unexpected virtues of the foreigner a rebuke to him and his countrymen. Thus Brocardus, praising the good points of Saracens and Nestorians, shakes his head over the shortcomings of European Christians. Mandeville makes this a major theme: "Alas," he cries, "that it is great slander to our faith and to our law, when folk that be without law shall reprove us and undername us of our sins" (ch. 15). Under the strain of accommodating to unfamiliar ways, the discomforts and dangers of travel, and the anxiety of being away from home, the virtues of the foreigner stand out ironically in relief, turning us back on ourselves.

Chaucer employs this double-edged quality of travellers' observations. He is in no foreign land but in his own. His fellow pilgrims are familiar English types; nothing is strange but their idiosyncrasies and their stories. The narrator's unfailing enthusiasm for all of them, good and bad alike, is "ironic," so we infer that Chaucer himself is castigating the wicked ones. But is he? We see the shortcomings of the Friar, say, or the Shipman or Pardoner because we share with the author a knowledge of his society, certain stereotypes of good and evil behavior, and a set of standards for judging morality. Yet nowhere does Chaucer's own indignation come out directly, like Gower's in the *Confessio* or *Vox clamantis*. Chaucer masks his own reactions. We say it is a matter of tone—yes. Here and there we suspect indignation on his part, but it is never expressed. Guessing it from the tone is part of the game. But Chaucer turns the tables even here. In the masquerade of the literal-minded, gregarious pilgrim he plays a kind of Holy Fool who stumbles into Christian charity as if by mistake. We perceive his dim-wittedness, but his simpleton's charity infects us all the same: it makes us see the created man beneath the canker evil, puts us in mind that we should look to our own sins first and not presume to judge the sins of others.[12]

But Chaucer adds to this point-counterpoint one feature carefully prepared for from the start. The pilgrims come within sight of the shrine, the shadows of the day are falling; there is but one tale left, the Parson's. Everything "modern" in the work—its verisimilitude, its attention to individual character, its literary gamesmanship, its self-consciousness about language and fictionality and art—all this is wiped away. In the final group of tales, the center will not hold: in the Canon's Yeoman's Tale we get a story of ideals betrayed and hopes dashed, in the Second Nun's Tale a real saint's legend, the only one in the work. In the last tale, the Manciple's, we get a fable that discredits tale-telling and language and art itself, makes Phoebus Apollo a cuckold, turns the primeval white crow to black, takes away his ability to speak because he told the truth, and ends by commending silence. Then the Parson's "meditation" in prose, a work of a wholly different kind from anything that has gone before. This does not mean *The Canterbury Tales* is "two books"; it is one book whose ending demands of us a different frame of mind and a different kind of reading.

12. This is, as I tried to show in "Chaucer the Man," *PMLA* 80 (1965): 337–343, a Christian and Augustinian idea; Augustine's famous dictum (*City of God,* 14. 6) was that one should hate the vice but love the man.

And if we meet this demand, we must change our estimate of the whole. Those who *must* have their genial, ironic Chaucer must avert their eyes from these earnest and severe elements at the end.

Perhaps this quality of the ending explains why critics have clung so tenaciously to the idea that there was to be a whole return journey, a homecoming and a prize supper. The pilgrimage, as we have seen, was normally conceived as a one-way journey and was so described. If Chaucer had finished the work on the model of pilgrimage narratives, he would have described the various "pilgrimages" to shrines in Canterbury, chiefly of course to the martyr's tomb, and at the most would have alluded to the return. Not that he wasn't ahead of his time in the art of describing a pilgrimage—quarrels and thievery and the seamy side of behavior really come to the fore only in fifteenth-century accounts of pilgrimages—so he could have been ahead of his time in providing a homecoming. But there is no evidence of it. We *have* the quarrels and the seamy side; we do *not* have the return journey, not even the arrival at the shrine, but only a typological Pisgah sight from which the promised land can be seen but not reached before death. Hence we should understand, as readers did until the middle of the nineteenth century, that the journey takes place unrealistically in one day: the gathering darkness of the Parson's Prologue signals the end of the life of man. What we have in the ending of *The Canterbury Tales* is the unworldly aspect of pilgrimage, the metaphor and the idea.

Chaucer did so much that was new that it is hard, five centuries later, to realize how in the end he fell back on

the old. It is not hard to realize that he anticipated here
the rejection of medieval religion, the whole complex
of Crusades, relics, indulgences, saints, miracles, that
was to pass away a century later. He embodied that
complex not just in the pilgrimage frame but in the
body of the work, in the pilgrims themselves and in
their tales. The first pilgrim described, the Knight, is a
Crusader "late y-come from his viage" and has been
throughout his career a worthy soldier of fortune, a
follower of the military movements of his day: a mod-
est, idealistic, admirable member of a class that has
ceased to scrutinize its values, a figure rather like "Sir
John Mandeville" himself in his self-portrayal. His son
the Squire, more a follower of courtly fads, whose one
experience in battle has been the embarrassing
"crusade" of 1383 to Flanders (it was little better than a
pillaging expedition), serves up for his tale a complex
slice of the "matter of Araby" with Mandevillian details about the court of the Great Khan; his tale is the
one place where direct influence from Mandeville is
likely. The Wife of Bath has been on the Jerusalem
pilgrimage three times, and to other shrines; the Pardoner is selling indulgences to those who will venerate
his admittedly false relics. The Second Nun tells a
saint's legend, the Prioress a miracle of the Blessed
Virgin (in which the natural villainy of Jews is taken as
a donnée). There are types of clerics in need of reform
(the Monk, the Friar), corrupt ecclesiastical officers
(the Summoner and Pardoner, who travel together).
The moral tales told on the pilgrimage are chiefly
told by pilgrims whose own morality is open to
question—the Man of Law and the Physician, for

example. And, since travelling for fun or curiosity was the sinful antithesis to "true" pilgrimage, the tale-telling game itself is a corruption. Indeed in virtually all the tales one could find some kind of travel that an ingenious critic might take for minipilgrimages or antipilgrimages that mimic the frame of the whole.

In all of this perhaps *we* can see the handwriting on the wall. But in the end Chaucer embraced that obsolescent complex in its old, ideal form. This clash of old ideals and present actualities evokes a reaction difficult for us to grasp; hence we must fumble with "models," comparisons, analogues, in order to feel our way back into Chaucer's idea. If we are to get even a glimmer of what the work was meant to be in its own time, we must learn a sensibility that has long since disappeared. For in the end Chaucer was trying to recapture some of that humanism of the thirteenth century—which was the humanism of Dante—that believed it was possible to gather all experience and all knowledge into a single whole. He meant to have arranged his pilgrimage of this world as Boethius suggests Philosophy has done: to have "woven me with thy resouns the house of Dedalus, so entrelaced that it is unable to be unlaced," to have "folded together (by replicatioun of words) a manner wonderful cercle of environing of the simplicite divine" (III. Pr. 12).

I am repeating here what I argued, in another book, was Chaucer's idea of *The Canterbury Tales*. There I tried to make it clear that I was undertaking a historical inquiry and felt myself under the necessity of demonstrating that any ideas or figures or models I attributed to the poet—the labyrinth, the interlace, the unilinear pilgrimage, or whatever—were *in actual fact* known to him, were present in his thoughts because they are explicitly present in his writings. I hope I made it clear that I think such a historical inquiry a difficult undertaking and am well aware I may be wrong; but I am, anyway, attempting to deal in historical facts, not imaginings and not "phenomenology." Part of Chaucer's idea was to invite various reactions from various readers—precisely as he *shows* various reactions of the pilgrims to one another and one another's tales. In our time, this fact about Chaucer's work, that the presence of the reader's self is necessary to any true reading of it, unnerves many and altogether unhinges some: they want "the reader" to be an objectively verifiable entity fabricated and relentlessly policed by the author, as some formalist critics used to want "the narrator" to be a literary creation scientifically verifiable from "the text itself," and surgically removable from the writer's self. When a critic deviates from these rigidities, he is scolded for projecting his private fantasies upon the author, or told that he is "making earnest of game" (finding meaning where presumably a virgin meaninglessness was intended), or charged with "inconsistency."

But Chaucer had inherited from the tradition of travel and pilgrimage writings a form that had evolved naturally—one that invited vicarious participation and personal reaction from the reader, an open-ended form that allowed the reader to believe or doubt as he saw fit, to be fascinated or repelled, skeptically "distanced" or imaginatively involved. In dealing with such a form, consistency can only be foolish consistency. When we read such books of travel we invoke standards of verifiable fact on the one hand while we weigh hearsay evidence on the other. What is interesting and amazing in such books must be in conflict with what is unimpeachably factual—the bananas pilgrims described are credible enough, but the crucifix they saw in a banana cut crosswise (and lengthwise too) is what makes good reading. Our reactions, which vary according to our frames of mind, become part of the experience of reading such works: if we do not in some measure project our private thoughts upon the author, we are not reading with the fascination the author presupposed. That he intended us to react does not mean he intended us all to react in the same way.

Ideas about literature change as all ideas do, and Chaucer's idea of a literary idea was something he struggled with and wrote about.[13] His notion is grounded in medieval ideas about literature and art, but there are differences that bring Chaucer closer to us than most of his contemporaries. He seems to have felt that poetic invention was partly reliant on chance or luck: *inventio* was, as its etymology suggests, finding something, not just deciding on a plan. And, as he makes plain in *The House of Fame,* one finds a poetic idea among "tidings." Tidings are news—events told and reported (there is an off chance that the word was his translation of Italian *novelle*). He makes it clear that a tiding is a tiding whether it is true or false: there can be many tidings of one event and tidings of non-events.

13. My afterthoughts about this were kindly invited by E. T. Donaldson, and published as "Chaucer's Idea of an Idea," *Essays and Studies,* n.s., 29 (1976): 39–55.

Tidings are where events and language meet, where the world becomes preserved in words. They are the end of action; they are the beginnings of legends and fictions, the raw stuff of literature. Chaucer came to be interested in the uniqueness and delimitedness, the puzzling authenticity of each personage and each tiding, and the randomness with which tidings are heard and reiterated. From this point of view, each of the Canterbury tales is a tiding: not each is true but each is authentic—each has a person behind it even if that person is a liar. We have to seek out and decide upon the truth or authenticity of tidings, and so reading literature demands of us an act of will: the truth of a poem, if it is written "for our doctrine," must be in *our* idea of it.

This idea of a literary idea was risky and theatrical, "distanced," highly disciplined. It calls upon a frame of mind in us, anticipates that frame of mind and in part inculcates it. It is not a "strategy": strategy is a military metaphor—strategy implies manipulation. It is rather a stance, that invites and permits. It deflects our attention to *seeming:* to the author's or narrator's mind, or to one character's mind, and always in some measure to the reader's mind. The basis of its verisimilitude is not in "going direct to life" as used to be thought, but in its aura of the unknown and the unknowable. For tidings have the power to create random impressions, each equally real to the one that holds that impression. And this randomness is the ultimate irony: that despite the poet's purpose and the reader's good will, nothing can be counted on to mean what it seems.

This ultimate irony is what puts the realistic fiction in Chaucer on a footing with the ideal or allegorical fiction. The nature of fictions has become a major issue of our time and is likely to remain so, for we habitually address the issue by asking about the relation of fiction to reality, knowing we are quite a bit less certain than former ages were that we know what is real. J. V. Cunningham has spoken of the tale of the patient Griselda as an "ideal fiction," a presentation of "the extreme case."[14] The extreme case is what the figural or ideal presentation shares with the realistic one. The Prioress's brooch is not less an extreme case than Griselda's patience. It dangles from her beads, shining in gold, with its crowned A and its "Amor vincit omnia"—ornamental, elegant, aristocratic, secular and religious at once as best we can divine—telling us something too complex and too objective to pin down. Such attention to detail is almost sacramental: in such details we conceive a meaning beyond what is evident to the senses. Chaucer invites us to surmise that this meaning is available to a detailed examination of objective reality, though after a century of Chaucer scholarship it turns out it is not. He would have surmised that it is known to God, that it has ultimate reality. Such ideas of an objective or an ultimate reality may seem no longer possible, yet we cannot shake them off. We continue to understand and justify our fictions in relation to them, even if those objective and ultimate realities are fictions too.

14. "Ideal Fiction," *Shenandoah* 19 (Winter, 1968): 38–41.

5.
Travellers and Readers

By the end of the fifteenth century the pilgrimage was in decline; by the end of the sixteenth century its important medieval associations—Crusades, indulgences, relics—had disappeared or changed their character in Catholic thought. While people went, as they still do, to shrines and on journeys to holy places, the enterprise was no longer central in European culture. When Erasmus accompanied Sir Thomas More and John Colet on the Canterbury pilgrimage ca. 1515 and described the experience with distaste (the Saint would have been better pleased had his riches been given to the poor, he has Colet suggest to the priest at the shrine, to the priest's horror) he was echoing a feeling common among the enlightened.

Reform and counter-reform were parts of a single historic movement: it did not take Protestantism to bring the pilgrimage to an end—the complex of medieval institutions to which it was central was crying out for reform already in Chaucer's time. But for Protestant England that complex was more decisively finished by the seventeenth century than on the continent. Looking back on it as a thing of the past, no one summed it up more penetratingly than John Milton in

Book III of *Paradise Lost,* describing the "Paradise of Fools" or "Limbo of Vanities":

> . . . Eremites and Friars
> White, Black and Grey, with all thir trumpery.
> Here Pilgrims roam, that stray'd so far to seek
> In Golgotha him dead, who lives in Heav'n;
> And they who to be sure of Paradise
> Dying put on the weeds of Dominic,
> Or in Franciscan think to pass disguis'd;
> . . . .
> . . . then might ye see
> Cowls, Hoods and Habits with thir wearers tost
> And flutter'd into Rags, then Reliques, Beads,
> Indulgences, Dispenses, Pardons, Bulls,
> The sport of Winds . . .
>
> (474–480, 489–493)

What Milton is really describing is the interiorization of religious experience. Physical things—relics, costumes, travel—were part of medieval religion to an extent no longer true anywhere by Milton's time. But to the Protestant—and especially the Puritan—mentality, there was a special horror in the physical aspects of religion: even the metaphor of journey had to be interiorized. And indeed *Paradise Lost* ends with Adam and Eve embarking—for all mankind—on life's pilgrimage (the last word of the poem, "way," was by tradition associated with pilgrimage):

> The world was all before them, where to choose
> Thir place of rest, and Providence thir guide:
> They hand in hand with wand'ring steps and slow,
> Through Eden took thir solitary way.

Day-to-day life lived in unremitting moral consciousness is the only pilgrimage left.

In England, interest in continental travel, once it was
in this way divorced from the old complex of religious
institutions, became married to humanism. It took the
form of the "grand tour," an educational journey
rather much like the literary and historical pilgrimage
Petrarch had recommended; and like Petrarch's, it was
primarily a voyage through Italy, of the kind Milton
made at the age of thirty (and not unlike the two
Chaucer had made, at thirty and thirty-five, though he
did not make them for that purpose). One would suppose that those young Englishmen, off to cultural
shrines, might have called themselves pilgrims by
analogy, but I don't find that they did so. They were
travelling to learn, not to worship. Hence their experience didn't have the one-way character of the medieval
pilgrimage: their purpose was to bring knowledge and
experience home for future use, very different from
getting an indulgence. Their journeys could never
have been declared complete *at* their destination, as
pilgrimages had been. Nor could they have been
reckoned a metaphor for the whole of human life.

But the humanistic tour inherited from the old pilgrimages its essence of curiosity, once a sinful temptation, now an intellectual virtue; in this respect it was
cousin to the Renaissance voyages of exploration and
conquest, whose medieval ancestry had been in mercantile and missionary voyages to the Far East like
those described by Marco Polo, William of Ru-
brouquis, or Friar Odoric (all of whom continued to be
known—they are cited often by Purchas). Mandeville,

describing his travels, makes the first part a Jerusalem pilgrimage; but the second part is oriental exploration and adventure, and—though religion was still much on his mind, though his journey led him like a pilgrim to the land of Prester John and to the unapproachable Earthly Paradise—he never applies any of the language of pilgrimage to it, even figuratively.

The explorers who crossed the Atlantic took along their copies of Mandeville for any facts the old book might provide; and their motives were tinged with religious considerations—converting the heathen, or finding the Earthly Paradise, captured their imaginations along with conquest, gold, spices, trade routes, and the sheer interest of strange lands. But they clearly understood that their travels were different in kind from pilgrimages. They too were bringing back something, goods or information; they had no destination comparable to a shrine; their journeys were no metaphor for human life. On the contrary, no voyage of exploration was complete if the explorers did not survive and get back home. The old pilgrims' notion that it would be a special grace to die in Jerusalem was inimical to the explorers: their true destination was their starting point. They were for this reason not given to calling themselves pilgrims. It was only when the pilgrimage had disappeared as an institution that a writer like Samuel Purchas could think of "pilgrimage" as an image of travel in general.

If there were any exception to this, one would expect to find it in Columbus's logbooks and letters. He was the first, and perhaps on that account the most fantastic and fanatical, of the Renaissance explorers,

and is the most puzzling. Religion loomed large
among his motives: above all, or so he said, he wished
to convert the heathen. And indeed Columbus's third
voyage did take in his mind something like the form of
a pilgrimage. He believed he had arrived at the Earthly
Paradise: by all authorities it was at the easternmost
end of the *orbis terrarum*—"the end of the East." Mandeville, in his thirty-third chapter, approaching
Paradise from the Orient, had found it "so high that it
toucheth nigh to the circle of the moon," enclosed by a
moss-covered wall having one entrance barred by fire,
"so that no man that is mortal ne dare not enter."
Columbus must have read this passage many times
and thought very hard about approaching the end of
the East from the west, as he had deduced he would do.
For he hatched the theory, not so improbable by
medieval standards, that the earth was not round after
all (as everyone knew it was) but pear shaped; that atop
the earth (at the equator), closest to heaven, was a pro-
tuberance, which he compared to a woman's breast;
and that the nipple of this breast was the Earthly
Paradise.[1] Let Freudians observe that he understood
what paradise really is; it was, anyway, his idea of
where he had been. Oddly, the idea seems to have
made little impression back in Spain, even upon the
pious Queen Isabella. But Columbus himself, hold-

1. *The Four Voyages of Christopher Columbus,* ed. and trans. J. M.
Cohen (Baltimore: Penguin Books, 1969), pp. 217–219. See
Samuel Eliot Morison, *Admiral of the Ocean Sea: A Life of Chris-
topher Columbus* (Boston: Little, Brown, 1942), pp. 556–558, and
Edmundo O'Gorman, *The Invention of America* (Bloomington,
Ind.: Indiana University Press, 1961), pp. 97–99.

ing this essentially religious conception about his destination—and quite capable of comparing the New World to a tit—seems never to have thought of comparing his voyage to a pilgrimage.

The voyages of migration were different: they were, like pilgrimages, one-way journeys. And some such voyages, like that to Massachusetts, were made out of religious motives. But on the testimony of the *OED* the term *pilgrim* was used only by the Massachusetts colonists and wasn't applied to other early settlers until later. Writing in 1630, ten years after the landing at Plymouth, Governor Bradford used the word, alluding to Hebrews 9:13, a text that must have touched the colonists deeply:

These all died in faith, not having received the promises, but having seen them afar off, and were persuaded of them, and embraced them, and confessed that they were strangers and pilgrims on the earth. For they that say such things declare plainly that they seek a country. And truly, if they had been mindful of that country from whence they came out, they might have had opportunity to have returned. But now they desire a better country, that is, a heavenly.

What Bradford wrote was that the settlers "knew they were but pilgrims" and lifted their eyes "to the heavens, their dearest country"—a reference to the metaphor of pilgrimage. Some seventy years later, Cotton Mather, no doubt with the same scriptural text in mind, wrote that the settlers "found a New World . . . in which they found they must live like strangers and pilgrims." Evidently the usage was more or less common and had more or less continuity, but none of those who used it suggest that the New World was itself the promised land or the heavenly country. (That fancy appears to have been reserved for the westward migrants who named the Golden Gate, presumably, after the one in Jerusalem through which Jesus had entered the city—a mode of hyperbole that still exists in California, the "Golden State.") The notion that the early New England settlers, and by extension all early settlers in America, were pilgrims or pilgrim fathers became standard by the middle of the nineteenth century and remains part of the popular iconography of Thanksgiving Day into the present. The earliest meaning of this notion seems to have suggested a one-way journey with a religious motive and eschatological expectations, a sense quite true to the old idea of pilgrimage. I don't believe it developed any overtones of the Puritan or Protestant ethic, as the image of pilgrimage did in eighteenth-century fiction. If anything, it became fixed and its original overtones lost, at least if one may judge from a sentence in the *Daily Chronicle* of 1903 that mentions "one of the original 'Canterbury pilgrims', as the first settlers in the New England province founded under the auspices of the Church of England were styled."

While the medieval pilgrimage left only such traces on other kinds of travel, it kept its character in the minds of readers.

How many medieval accounts of pilgrimages were known in England after the Reformation, it is hard to say. The discovery of the New World captured public imagination and seemingly drove out the older interest in the Holy Land and its environs. (That Renaissance interest in exploring strange lands, which has lasted into our own time and is epitomized I suppose by the *National Geographic,* has been "driven out" in somewhat the same way by space travel: we transfer to space our interest in distant lands and then imagine space creatures similar to the sports of nature or the noble savages described by the older explorers.) The Holy Land and the Near East remained part of geography, at all events, and much of the traditional lore about them found its way into the great geographical collections and "relations" of the Renaissance.[2] Of these, Hakluyt's *Principal Navigations, Voyages, and Discoveries of the English Nation* (1598–1600), widely known, is the most famous and very much a product of its age. Hakluyt's interest was in geography, and his geographical materials, for example his descriptions of botanical life, shade off into the new science. But he had these interests because they were useful to trade and colonization; he was at base preaching imperialism.[3] His successor, Purchas, was more of a journalist (much reviled in modern times for omitting the dull parts of the material he inherited from Hakluyt and throwing the documents away). Both were clergymen, but Purchas was the more religious; his *Pil-*

2. See H. S. Bennett, *English Books and Readers 1475 to 1557* (Cambridge, England: Cambridge University Press, 1952), pp. 120–123, and its subsequent volumes, covering 1558–1603 (1965), pp. 205–214, and 1605–1640 (1970), pp. 167–172.

3. Louis B. Wright, *Middle-Class Culture in Elizabethan England* (Chapel Hill: University of North Carolina Press, 1935), pp. 524–533.

grimage has been called a "theological geography," as its subtitle suggests.[4] On this score he was closer to the Middle Ages than Hakluyt and others, and it was he, after all, who envisaged all travels as pilgrimages and all travellers as pilgrims.

Some Renaissance travel writers went to the Holy Land and the Near East, but not as pilgrims. A book of great popularity was George Sandys's *A Relation of a Journey* (1615); its subtitle styles it "a description of the Turkish empire, of Egypt, of the Holy Land, of the remote parts of Italy and islands adjoining"—very much like the old accounts of pilgrimages, save that the journey was for research, not worship. The book appeared in new editions in 1621, 1627, 1632, and 1637.[5] A similar book by William Lithgow, published in 1614, was called *A Most Delectable, And True Discourse, of an admired and painefull peregrination from Scotland, to the most famous Kingdomes in Europe, Asia and Affricke;* it contains a detailed account of a pilgrimage in the Holy Land, the author expressing impatience with the institution and, in the good old tradition of pilgrimage writings, with his fellow pilgrims (but, too, with most foreigners). He recited a psalm, and wept, on seeing Jerusalem. That he used the word *peregrination* in his title is little more than a coincidence, for by his time the word had lost all associations with pilgrimage—it meant "travelling." Still, in his dedicatory epistle to Charles I he refers to his travels as a pilgrimage. Lithgow, who said he travelled by foot ("my pilgrimage was ever pedestrial"), kept adding to

4. Ibid., p. 537.
5. Ibid., p. 545.

his book—it came out in five more printings during his lifetime—and it seems to have enjoyed an enduring popularity: it appeared in what purported to be a twelfth edition in 1814.[6]

Of such travel books as these, which contained accounts of the Jerusalem pilgrimage, Mandeville's remained popular into our time—is probably, all told, the most widely known of all such books. In England—to say nothing of its wide circulation on the continent—it was first printed in 1496 and at least once again before 1500; there were at least four printings in the sixteenth century, and there have been some dozen or more every hundred years since then.[7] How widely any of these printings was circulated, how widely the book was read, how carefully, or by what segment of the population are matters very hard to determine. And even if we had such statistics, we would not know what place Mandeville's book held in the consciousness of various centuries. Anecdotal evidence alone can bring us up short: Shakespeare "echoes" it, Coleridge read it avidly, George Eliot quotes it as an epigraph to a chapter in *Middlemarch*. In the seventeenth century, Hakluyt, who had printed it in his first edition, replaced it in his second with three of its sources:[8] from

6. Ibid., p. 547.

7. Bennett, *Rediscovery of Sir John Mandeville*, pp. 346–359. There are other editions undated, and doubtless others unknown. Mrs. Bennett says on p. 254 that "while ten editions satisfied the seventeenth century, the eighteenth absorbed at least twice that number," but the figure doesn't agree with the seventeenth- and eighteenth-century printings she lists on pp. 349–356, eleven each in the seventeenth and eighteenth centuries, fifteen in the nineteenth—another of the many little puzzles in her book.

8. Ibid., pp. 245–246.

this time it seems to have been understood that Mandeville had borrowed material from others, that his book was "stuffed with fables," that he was a typical exaggerating traveller. But he always had defenders; Purchas believed the true text of his work had been lost, Coleridge that its fables were "monkish interpolations." Sir Thomas Browne, with his usual common sense, thought that while it contained "impossibilities," it deserved to be read because "to a pregnant invention [it] may afford commendible mythology."[9] It was almost always accompanied by pictures, a tradition going back to the drawings in manuscripts and the woodcuts in the edition printed by Wynkyn de Worde. And very likely from the seventeenth century through the nineteenth it was more often read by children than by adults. But it was none the less important for that; the books we read in childhood and adolescence have a different—perhaps deeper—place in consciousness than the books we read as adults. To children everything is strange and possible; "impossibilities" do not bother them. This quality of wonder was, I believe, what gave Mandeville's the edge over other such books as adult reading. His "impossibilities" and fables symbolized the uncharted world of the possible. While the New World was still being explored, people must have felt there was a chance that he was right after all—that there *was* a fountain of youth, that there *were* men whose heads do grow beneath their shoulders. That ambiguous area between the possible and the impossible nurtured the impulse to explore and the

9. Ibid., p. 252.

curiosity to study the New World. Mandeville's skeptical manner gave his book an essential appeal to the modern spirit: after all, skepticism involves not doubt alone but a corresponding openness to unconsidered possibilities. It was only in the nineteenth century, when the earth had been almost completely explored and possibilities were chiefly known, that Mandeville was written off as a fake. Until then his book was read, one can say, *as a fiction:* he was viewed as a writer, not as an impostor. That is how he should be viewed, for it is the nature of fiction to tease our sense of reality, to tell lies but claim for them an essence of human truth.

Such writings about travel, ready at hand, easily became allegorized. Any voyage might be a "pilgrimage of life," and so the *idea* of pilgrimage reentered travel literature. Such allegories shaped prose fiction. *The Pilgrim's Progress* is the classic of the genre. But there were many other Puritan spiritual guides and autobiographies[10]—and we have to remember how many readers *lived* by such exemplars, exactly as they *died* by the numerous treatises on "the art of dying." Scholars have studied the influence of such writings on early fiction—on *Robinson Crusoe, Clarissa, Rasselas,* the novels of Fielding, Smollett, Sterne. Life *was* a pilgrimage to such authors, as dying was an "art," and everything we do or should do in life was a step along the road to the ultimate destination of every pilgrim, the Heavenly Jerusalem. In the age of Puritanism and the Protestant ethic this became a matter of individual choice and conduct, sometimes of a quite practical and

10. Hunter, *The Reluctant Pilgrim,* chs. 2–4.

unallegorical kind. In eighteenth-century fiction, as
Ronald Paulson has shown, the hero or heroine, as a
pilgrim exiled from his personal state of paradisal in-
nocence, needed to "become a moral agent, prove and
educate himself, and win for himself a 'heaven' that
would have been out of the question if he had remained
in Eden."[11] Heroes like Tom Jones and Clarissa are
pilgrims of this kind, as is Peregrine Pickle (whose first
name needs no comment). And I suppose a vestige of
the pattern is retained in modern fiction. It was not a
mere accident of history that among the first "stream
of consciousness" novels were the nine by Dorothy
Richardson, published between 1915 and 1939, collec-
tively called *Pilgrimage*—very much a metaphor for
human life, as it would seem, since they describe her
own. The quest and the journey remain powerful
structuring images in a great many novels. Conrad, in
Heart of Darkness, has Marlow call his voyage into the
Congo "a weary pilgrimage amongst hints for night-
mares," and he goes on referring, with irony, to his
crew as "the pilgrims." If the journey goes one way
and ends with something comparable to enlightenment or grace, it *is* like a pilgrimage, though more
often, as in Conrad, the full meaning of the voyage
comes only when the traveller has returned home. The
journey out west or back east in American fiction, or
journeys to Europe in writers like James, keep the his-

11. Ronald Paulson, "The Pilgrimage and the Family: Structures in the Novels of Fielding and Smollett," in G. S. Rousseau
and P.-G. Boucé, eds., *Tobias Smollett: Bicentennial Essays Presented
to Lewis M. Knapp* (Oxford: Oxford University Press, 1971),
p. 67.

torical possibilities of the pilgrimage motif: the Pisgah sight may be a kind of anti-grace, but the pattern is still there. In Joyce's *Ulysses,* "the first pivotal book in English since *Paradise Lost,*"[12] the pattern is decisively abandoned in favor of an odyssey.

Of earlier pilgrimage writings that continued to be read in England the most popular, Mandeville's and Chaucer's, were the most literary, and these writers were the most acutely aware of the genre's satiric potential. Satires like More's *Utopia* and *Gulliver's Travels* really should be read with this in mind. The returned traveller, reporting with wide-eyed wonder what he has seen and experienced, can invite the skepticism or disapprobation of the reader without tipping his hand. Human foibles are never more palpable and absurd than when observed in foreign lands (unless perhaps in talking animals). And, too, as every traveller knows, what we see abroad invites comparison with behavior and customs back home, turns us upon ourselves. The circumstance is akin to the realization of pilgrims that their religious journeys were all too often a mockery: the intentions of the institution were subverted by curiosity, not to say by pilgrims carving their initials on shrines, swearing, stealing, telling tales. Follow that line of self-questioning and you have misanthropy— Gulliver raving against pride. The more humble spirit of self-questioning was more endemic to satire; Friar Felix the pilgrim, asking himself whether pilgrimages accomplish anything that talk couldn't accomplish, is not unlike Mandeville reporting the Sultan's condem-

12. Hugh Kenner, *Joyce's Voices* (Berkeley and Los Angeles: University of California Press, 1978), p. xii.

nation of Christian hypocrisies. The difference is that
we see Friar Felix's vested interest in preaching; with
Mandeville we are struck by the narrator's objectivity
and modesty, and with his own shame, knowing what
the Mohammedan said is true. Such masks became the
satirist's stock in trade, and the role of the observant
traveller on life's pilgrimage was already at hand as one
such mask.

Apart from its influence on writers of fiction and
satire, the idea of the Jerusalem pilgrimage exerted an
influence on the general or common reader until the
end of the nineteenth century. It was part of the
"background" of reading, part of what readers
brought to other books. In Catholic countries the stations (or "way") of the Cross was a vestige of the
Jerusalem pilgrimage preserved in the liturgy, and in
Protestant countries a similar survival might be dis-
cerned in education: children in Victorian England
were all taught the geography of the Holy Land as if it
were useful information.[13] The most widely read book
in Victorian England, after the Bible, was *Pilgrim's
Progress;* children read it as a story, with no idea that it
was an allegory, and remembered it all their lives.[14]

13. Richard D. Altick, *The English Common Reader: A Social
History of the Mass Reading Public, 1800–1900* (Chicago: University
of Chicago Press, 1957), p. 154. Cf. E. S. Shaffer, *"Kubla Khan" and
"The Fall of Jerusalem": The Mythological School in Biblical Criticism
and Secular Literature, 1770–1800* (Cambridge, England: Cam-
bridge University Press, 1975), p. 61: "As Coleridge noted,
Jerusalem was Jesus's special care. . . . The intimate geography of
Jerusalem may serve as a Brunonian 'art of memory' to recall
Christ's life. But the symbolic presence is also an absence."

14. Altick, pp. 255–56.

Travel books enjoyed a steady popularity—a tabula-
tion made in 1838 put them second only to novels
among the contents of circulating libraries.[15] And
Robinson Crusoe, with its subliminal pilgrimage motif,
was always popular. In artistic and learned circles reading was wider and more arcane, but even the most
sophisticated adult reader would have read such books
as these in youth. They were part of the temper of the
times.

Probably this fact, rather than new scholarship, accounts for the manner in which Chaucer's *Canterbury
Tales* was understood until the nineteenth century.
Those who wrote of *The Canterbury Tales* mention
again and again the originality of its conception, the
realistic delineation of its characters, the variety of the
tales, the author's descriptive powers, and so on; we
may think them naive, but they were anyway reading
the work for what it is, not for what it might have
been. Among earlier critics, at least among those
selected by Derek Brewer in his recent two volumes[16]
and whatever others I know, there seems never to have
been any preoccupation with the unfinished quality of
The Canterbury Tales. The idea that Chaucer meant to
write the work according to the Host's plan, that he
meant to add links describing the progress of the journey in minute detail, and add sixty more tales for the
return to London, having each pilgrim tell two tales on
each leg of the journey and actually ending the work
with the projected supper at the Tabard, seems to be

15. Ibid., pp. 217–18.
16. *Chaucer: The Critical Heritage* (London: Routledge and
Kegan Paul, 1978).

chiefly an invention of the nineteenth century.[17] Until then, no one worried much about missing tales. I believe this was so in part because readers of those earlier times knew in their bones that a pilgrimage was quintessentially a one-way affair, that a homecoming wasn't part of the nature of the medieval pilgrimage. Nor does what was missing from *The Canterbury Tales* seem to have been much of a preoccupation until the *end* of the century, when critics began fretting over the number of days depicted and picking out tales Chaucer must have meant for the journey home.

Why? Partly because the nineteenth century was the age of novelistic realism. The new view of *The Canterbury Tales* was based on the premise that it is "true to life" like a novel. But, too, the nineteenth century was an age of grandiose artistic plans: it was pleasing to think of Chaucer's last work as a *cycle* of tales, vast in design. For Vast Designs in which the artist's reach exceeded his grasp, designs unfulfilled and elusive, like Wordsworth's *Recluse* or Marx's *Capital,* were also

17. Tyrwhitt in his "Introductory Discourse to the Canterbury Tales," printed in his edition of 1775, seems the first critic who offered a developed argument that the work is unfinished. He held that each pilgrim was meant to "tell at least one Tale in going to Canterbury, and another in coming back"; that the plan included, "probably, their adventures at Canterbury as well as upon the road"; that the tales would be connected with introductions; and that the prize supper would be the conclusion. He remarked once that some difficulties could be avoided by considering that the journey took more than one day, but did not really propose this. Furnivall (1868) was the chief begetter of the notion that the journey took three and a half days, that each pilgrim was meant to tell two tales either way, and so on. Skeat (1894) accepted Furnivall's notions tentatively. The mountain of conjectures is the product of our own busy century.

much in vogue—along with a few that were achieved, like Wagner's *Ring* or Proust's novel. The impulse that accounts for Coleridge's "Kubla Khan," with its appended note about the poet's dream during which he seemed to have composed a poem many times its length, may be precisely the impulse that made readers believe Chaucer's work was a mere fragment of a Vast Design that had existed in the pleasure dome of his imagination.

The result has been that in our time students of Chaucer have had to "discover," slowly, tentatively, that the pilgrimage frame of *The Canterbury Tales* is not after all local color but an allegory or metaphor of human life, at base religious. To some, this seems to make *The Canterbury Tales* abstract and dogmatic. But the antinomy belongs to us, not to the Middle Ages. The work, like medieval art in general, is at once realistic and abstract.[18] We can have it both ways. A real live pilgrimage to any medieval man *was* a metaphoric one-way journey to the Heavenly Jerusalem, and none the less real for that.

Readers of the nineteenth century could have known this from their reading better than other post-medieval readers: during the second half of the century interest in the medieval pilgrimage was renewed in England and on the continent, producing a

18. See Edgar De Bruyne, *The Esthetics of the Middle Ages,* trans. Eileen B. Hennessy (New York: Frederick Ungar, 1969), pp. 40–41 and passim; De Bruyne comments (p. 162) that "a literary work is beautiful by virtue of the direct or indirect radiance of the emotionally experienced physical or moral truths it contains. This, in our opinion, is the fundamental principle of the medieval esthetics of art."

large body of printed sources, among them the remarkable bibliography by Röhricht (1890) cited earlier. Accounts of pilgrimages were collected in England by Thomas Wright (*Early Travels in Palestine,* 1848), in Leipzig by J. C. M. Laurent (1864) and Titus Tobler (1874). In London the Palestine Pilgrims' Trust produced in fourteen volumes the Library of the Palestine Pilgrims Text Society (1887–1897). There were editions and translations done all over Europe, increased travel to the Holy Land, archeological expeditions; Renan's *Vie de Jésus* (1863) was begun when its author, on an archeological dig to the Holy Land, went about the holy places of Jesus's life as medieval pilgrims had done. Herman Melville (who read Mandeville, Sandys, and Wright) went to the Holy Land in 1857 and used his pilgrim's experience in his poem *Clarel.*

But then, when so many of the works had been collected and translated, they lost interest. At the turn of the century a new version of the Middle Ages, *our* version, took shape, and interest turned elsewhere. One might call this new version "the Third Medievalism."

The First Medievalism would have been the antiquarianism of the Renaissance, which looked back with ambivalent nostalgia and distaste upon that former age; Spenser's *Faerie Queene* and Milton's plan to write an epic of King Arthur would be emblematic of its positive side—indeed, the term *Middle Ages,* what came in the middle between antiquity and modernity, was its creation. The works of Hakluyt and Purchas belonged to the First Medievalism.

The <u>Second Medievalism</u> arose in the seventeenth century, with the study of history and language. It was to the Middle Ages what Renaissance humanism had been to classical antiquity. It sought out texts and practiced philology, which is the science of texts and their languages. At the same time it fostered an imaginative, romanticized search for the life and spirit of a former age. On this latter end of the spectrum Macpherson's three epics "translated" from fabricated medieval Gaelic poets and Chatterton's poems by his fabricated fifteenth-century poet "Thomas Rowley" are the more zany monuments, but there are, too, the novels and the scholarship of Sir Walter Scott. Under Scott's aegis philologists like Sir Frederic Madden uncovered and published medieval works hitherto unread, like *Sir Gawain and the Green Knight*. And during this period *Beowulf* and other vernacular poems of its stature became classics. The crowning achievements of the Second Medievalism were the great editions of the nineteenth century; the philological and linguistic scholarship that culminated in the appearance of the *OED;* the first histories of the Middle Ages; and, too, the creation of the great historical constructs—"the chivalric code," "courtly love," "the dark ages," "feudalism."

The <u>Third Medievalism</u> emerged at the close of the nineteenth century; that was when *our* Middle Ages took shape. It was an effort to evaluate and interpret the achievements of the Second Medievalism and to challenge its constructs, and was in large measure therefore a reaction. But it was also a new set of fashions. For example, the English morality play *Every-*

man, known as a text and a specimen, was produced in
1901 by the Elizabethan Stage Society—the first recorded production since the seventeenth century—on
a double bill with *The Sacrifice of Isaac* from the Chester
Cycle. The production was a great critical and popular
success, and other productions of other plays followed. *Everyman* reentered the realm of living theater
and rose above other morality plays as the classic of
its genre. It enjoyed an enormous vogue—it tells us
something that the first titles of Everyman's Library
appeared in 1905. Or again, until this time *Sir Gawain
and the Green Knight* was hardly viewed as more than
another medieval romance, interesting as evidence
of language and of "manners and customs" but not
generally acknowledged as a masterpiece, partly because of its difficulty. A new edition of it, by Israel
Gollanz, was made in 1897. In the same year it was
translated by Jessie Weston; it was she who popular-
ized it (her later study *From Ritual to Romance,* en-
shrined in T. S. Eliot's *The Waste Land,* is another
monument of the Third Medievalism). *Sir Gawain*
still received almost no critical attention until the
1930s, in fact none worth speaking of until the
1950s.[19] Today it is the classic of medieval English
romances—universally anthologized, translated and
edited countless times, and scrutinized beyond recognition.

In the study of Chaucer, Skeat's great edition was
completed in 1897, and Eleanor Prescott Hammond's
Chaucer: A Bibliographical Manual, which might be
called the great rooted blossomer of Chaucer schol-

19. See Steven Eric Levitsky, "The Discovery of *Sir Gawain
and the Green Knight*" (Ph.D. diss., Johns Hopkins, 1972).

arship, was published in 1908. Modern Chaucer studies date from these two works, which codify the learning and opinions of the nineteenth century into the *idées fixes* of the twentieth. It's instructive to note Mrs. Hammond's headings for her treatment of *The Canterbury Tales:* "Stories in a Framework," "Headlinks and Endlinks," "The Host," "The 'Fragments,'" "Evidence as to the Arrangement of the Tales," "The Order of the Tales," and so on. It is everywhere assumed that a Vast Design for a realistic work lies here in shards. We learn that until Furnivall (1868) critics spoke as if the journey took place all on one day, whereas now it is reckoned to last three and a half days; that until Wright (1847) critics assumed Chaucer knew the *Decameron,* whereas now it is acknowledged that there is no evidence he had seen it.[20] Those notions, emerging at the end of the Second Medievalism, became the dogmas of the Third.

One could pile up many more instances of this change, and one could ask whether there is now a Fourth Medievalism taking shape; but all of this falls outside our purpose.[21] The earlier version of the Mid-

20. Pp. 161, 152. Cf. my argument in *The Idea of the Canterbury Tales,* pp. 165–168, that the journey takes place on one symbolic day.

21. To my knowledge, only what I call the Second Medievalism has been studied. The monumental inquiry is Lionel Gossman, *Medievalism and the Ideologies of the Enlightenment: The World and Work of La Curne de Sainte-Palaye* (Baltimore: Johns Hopkins University Press, 1968). Alice Chandler, in *A Dream of Order: The Medieval Ideal in Nineteenth-Century English Literature* (Lincoln, Nebraska: University of Nebraska Press, 1970), studies the failure of the Second Medievalism in its political and ideological aspects. On the Third Medievalism, see my expanded remarks in *University Publishing* (Spring 1980).

dle Ages included the accounts of travel and pilgrimage, which were until the turn of the century taken for
granted as part of the corpus of medieval writings and
were therefore part of the "context" of medieval literature. With the coming of the Third Medievalism, they
fell into the background, perhaps *out* of the
background. By the 1950s even Mandeville needed to
be "rediscovered." And even in the early 1960s the
notion that Chaucer meant to end *The Canterbury Tales*
where in fact he ended it—at, or just outside,
Canterbury—was a radical departure from the going
realistic or "novelistic" way of reading the work: it
was, if advanced at all, held out with tongs. Ralph
Baldwin, in *The Unity of the Canterbury Tales* (1955),
was the first to propose that the Canterbury pilgrimage "becomes, and this is the *sovrasenso,* the pilgrimage
of the life of man." In that "becomes" he was echoing
the older notion that Chaucer "changed his mind"
about the plan, and Baldwin then fell back upon the old
realistic reading by making the Parson's Tale into a
dramatic scene during which the pilgrims blush and
repent as their various sins are one by one touched
upon in the Parson's "sermon"—none of which is in
The Canterbury Tales at all. Not until 1964, as far as I
am aware, did anyone suggest that *The Canterbury
Tales* might be viewed against the background of pilgrimage narratives.[22]

If those narratives deserved only to be read as
background, they would need to be read by few. But

22. The suggestion was made by Morton W. Bloomfield, in
"Authenticating Realism and the Realism of Chaucer," *Thought* 39
(1964): 348 (rpt. in *Essays and Explorations,* see p. 188) and was the
inspiration of the present study.

some members of the genre stand in the foreground as its masterpieces; they deserve to be read for themselves. They came into existence not because their authors were pilgrims and observers and notetakers but because they were writers: they had the writer's gift of snatching small details and passing thoughts from oblivion, discerning in them the wonder posterity would warm to, centuries later, when the smallest moment of their travels would seem curious and golden in its own right.

Index

Compositor:	Interactive Composition Corp.
Printer:	Thomson-Shore, Inc.
Binder:	Thomson-Shore, Inc.
Text:	VIP Bembo
Display:	VIP Bembo
Cloth:	Holliston Roxite A 50267
Paper:	60 lb P&S laid B-32